D1733546

ISRAEL TRAVEL GUIDE 2023

The Ultimate Guide to Discovering the Best Places to Visit, Things to Do, and Must-Try Israel Experiences.

(Essential Travel Guide)

By Walden Caldwell

Table of Contents

Chapter 1:   Introduction

Overview of Israel's History and Culture

Geography and Climate

Tips on language, currency, and customs

Chapter 2:   Accommodations:

Options for hotels, hostels, guesthouses, and rental properties in Israel

Recommendations for budget, mid-range, and luxury accommodations in different parts of the country

Chapter 3:   Transportation

Options for getting around Israel ,
including public transportation, taxis,
rental cars, and tours

Chapter 4:   Food and Drink:

Overview of Israel cuisine and dining
options, including recommended
restaurants and local specialties

Tips on finding the best food and
drink experiences, such as local
markets, food tours, and cooking
classes

Chapter 5:   Activities and
Attractions:

Overview of the top things to do and
see in Israel , including museums,
landmarks, outdoor activities, and
cultural experiences

Tips on finding the best activities and
attractions, such as guided tours and
off-the-beaten-path experiences

Chapter 6:   Detailed information on popular tourist destinations, including Jerusalem, Tel Aviv, the Dead Sea, and the Galilee region

Chapter 7:   Special events and festivals

Chapter 8:   Traveling with kids and families

Kid-friendly attractions and activities
Tips for traveling with children

Chapter 9:   Shopping

Overview of the local shopping scene in Israel , including markets, boutiques, and souvenir shops

Chapter 10: Nightlife in Israel

Tips for Nightlife in Israel:

Overview of the local nightlife scene in Israel, including bars, clubs, and live music venues

Chapter 11: Practical Information

Tips on staying safe and healthy while traveling in Israel , including information on local laws and customs, medical facilities, and emergency resources

Information on visas, travel insurance

Tips for a successful and enjoyable trip

Chapter 12: Christian Pilgrimage in Israel

The most popular Christian pilgrimage sites in Israel include:

Chapter 13: Itineraries
Final thoughts and next steps

My First Visit to Israel

It was a dream come true as I stepped off the plane and onto the streets of Israel. I had always wanted to visit this holy land

and now, here I was, finally making my pilgrimage.

My first stop was Jerusalem, the heart of the holy land and the center of my spiritual journey. As I walked through the streets, the energy of the city was palpable. Everywhere I looked, there were reminders of the rich history and religious significance of this place.

I started my visit at the Church of the Holy Sepulchre, one of the most sacred sites in Christianity. As I walked through the ancient stone halls, I couldn't help but feel a sense of awe and reverence. The church is said to be built on the site of Jesus' crucifixion, burial, and resurrection and the atmosphere inside was electric with the energy of centuries of prayers and devotion.

The Western Wall, also known as the Wailing Wall, was my next stop. This is the last remaining wall of the Second Temple and it's a sacred site for Jewish people. I couldn't help but be moved by the sight of people from all walks of life, gathered here to pray and leave written prayers in the crevices of the wall.

I also had the opportunity to visit the Dome of the Rock, a beautiful and iconic Islamic shrine that sits on the Temple Mount. This is a site of great religious significance for Jews, Christians, and Muslims alike and it was amazing to see people of different faiths coming together in peace and respect.

The next day I took a day trip to the Sea of Galilee, where Jesus performed many of his miracles and where he called his first disciples. The first site I visited was the Church of the Multiplication of Loaves and Fishes, where Jesus is said to have fed the five thousand. The beautiful mosaics and frescoes inside the church were breathtaking.

I also had the opportunity to visit the Church of the Beatitudes, where Jesus delivered the Sermon on the Mount. The church is built on the traditional site where this event took place and the views from the church's terrace were breathtaking.

Finally, I climbed the Mount of Beatitudes, where Jesus delivered the Sermon on the Mount. The views from the top were incredible, and I felt a sense of peace and serenity wash over me as I took in the stunning panoramic views of the lake and the surrounding hills.

The next stop on my pilgrimage was Nazareth, where Jesus spent his childhood. The highlight of my visit was the Church of the Annunciation, which is built on the site where the Angel Gabriel is said to have appeared to the Virgin Mary. The church was beautiful, and I couldn't help but feel a sense of wonder and awe as I stood in the place where one of the most important events in Christian history is said to have occurred.

I also had the opportunity to visit the Jordan River, where Jesus was baptized by John the Baptist. The river was not as I had imagined, it was quite small and not as grand as I thought. But the energy of the place was undeniable, and I felt a sense of spiritual renewal as I dipped my toes in the water.

My last stop on my pilgrimage was Jerusalem, I also visited the Basilica of the Agony in Ein Karem and the Garden of Gethsemane, where Jesus was betrayed by Judas and arrested. The church is built on the traditional site where Jesus prayed in agony before his arrest, and the garden is home to ancient olive trees that are said to have been there at the time of Jesus' arrest. The peaceful and tranquil atmosphere of the garden was a fitting end to my pilgrimage.

Overall, my first visit to Israel was an experience I will never forget. The pilgrimage sites were incredibly powerful and moving, and I felt a deep sense of connection to the land and the history. I also enjoyed the local culture, food and the friendly people. My heart was filled with a sense of wonder and gratitude for the opportunity to experience this holy land. I will always remember my first visit to Israel as a transformative journey of faith and personal growth.

Chapter 1:   Introduction

Israel is a small country located in the Middle East, bordered by Lebanon to the north, Syria to the northeast, Jordan to the east, Egypt to the southwest, and the Mediterranean Sea to the west. It is a parliamentary democracy with a population of around 9 million people, the majority of whom are Jewish.

The history of Israel is long and complex, dating back to ancient times. The land of Israel has been inhabited by various peoples throughout history, including the Israelites, the Romans, the Byzantines, the Ottomans, and the British. In 1947, the United Nations voted to partition Palestine into separate Jewish and Arab states, and in 1948, Israel declared its independence.

Since its founding, Israel has been embroiled in conflicts with its Arab neighbors, including the 1948 Arab-Israeli War, the 1967 Six-Day War, and the ongoing

Israeli-Palestinian conflict. Despite these conflicts, Israel has managed to become a developed and prosperous country, with a strong economy and a high standard of living.

One of the main attractions of Israel is its rich cultural heritage. The country is home to a number of important religious sites, including the Western Wall and the Dome of the Rock in Jerusalem, the Church of the Holy Sepulchre in Jerusalem, and the Church of the Nativity in Bethlehem. Israel is also home to a number of ancient ruins, such as the Roman city of Caesarea and the Crusader castle at Acre.

Israel is also known for its beautiful beaches, great weather, and delicious food. The country is home to a diverse range of cuisines, including traditional Jewish cuisine, Mediterranean cuisine, and Middle Eastern cuisine. Visitors can enjoy fresh seafood, falafel, shawarma, and hummus, among many other delicious dishes.

In addition to its cultural and historical attractions, Israel is also a popular destination for outdoor activities. Visitors can explore the beautiful landscapes of the Negev Desert, hike in the Golan Heights, or swim in the Dead Sea, the lowest point on Earth.

Israel is also a popular destination for medical tourism. The country has an advanced medical infrastructure, and is known for its expertise in areas such as fertility treatments, cancer treatments, and orthopedic surgeries.

Israel is a fascinating country with a rich history, diverse culture, and beautiful natural landscapes. Whether you are interested in religious sites, ancient ruins, beaches, or outdoor activities, Israel has something to offer everyone. With a little bit of planning and preparation, you can have an unforgettable trip to Israel.

Overview of Israel's History and Culture

The history of Israel is a rich and complex tapestry that spans thousands of years. The land of Israel has been inhabited by various peoples throughout history, including the Israelites, the Romans, the Byzantines, the Ottomans, and the British.

The Israelites, also known as the Hebrews, are considered to be the earliest inhabitants of the land of Israel. According to the Bible, the Israelites were led out of slavery in Egypt by Moses and eventually settled in the land of Israel under the leadership of Joshua. The Israelites established a monarchy under King Saul, and later King David and King Solomon. However, after the death of King Solomon, the Israelite kingdom split into two: Israel in the north and Judah in the south.

The land of Israel was conquered by the Babylonians in 586 BCE, and the Israelites were exiled to Babylon. They returned to the land of Israel after the Persians conquered Babylon and allowed the Israelites to return to their homeland. This period is known as the Second Temple period and it was marked by the rebuilding of the Temple in Jerusalem.

In 63 BCE, the Roman Empire conquered the land of Israel and it became a province of the Roman Empire. During this period, the land of Israel saw a significant increase in the number of Jewish people and the emergence of Christianity.

In the 4th century CE, the Roman Empire adopted Christianity as its official religion and the land of Israel became a Christian territory. However, the Jewish people continued to practice their religion and maintain their distinct culture.

In the 7th century CE, the Arab Islamic empire conquered the land of Israel, and it became a part of the Islamic Caliphate. The land of Israel was ruled by various Islamic dynasties over the centuries, including the Umayyads, the Abbasids, and the Fatimids.

In the 12th century CE, the Crusaders invaded the land of Israel and established a Christian kingdom. However, the Crusaders were eventually driven out by the Muslim armies.

In the 16th century CE, the Ottoman Empire conquered the land of Israel and it became a province of the Ottoman Empire. The land of Israel remained under Ottoman rule for over four centuries, during which time the Jewish people experienced periods of persecution and discrimination.

In the late 19th and early 20th century, Jewish immigrants began to return to the land of Israel, a movement known as the Zionist movement, with the goal of establishing a Jewish homeland in the land of Israel. This movement gained momentum with the rise of anti-Semitism in Europe and the Holocaust.

In 1947, the United Nations voted to partition Palestine into separate Jewish and Arab states, and in 1948, Israel declared its independence. Since its founding, Israel has been embroiled in conflicts with its Arab neighbors, including the 1948 Arab-Israeli War, the 1967 Six-Day War, and the ongoing Israeli-Palestinian conflict.

Culture in Israel is a blend of the diverse cultures of its many immigrant groups, including Ashkenazi Jews, Sephardic Jews, Mizrahi Jews, Druze, and Palestinian Arabs. Israeli culture is characterized by a strong emphasis on education and a love of the arts. The country has a thriving theater scene and is home to many world-renowned musicians, dancers, and artists.

The Israeli cuisine is diverse and reflects the country's melting pot of cultures. The traditional Jewish cuisine is based on the Ashkenazi and Sephardic culinary traditions, and includes dishes such as gefilte fish, latkes, and matzah ball soup. Mediterranean cuisine is also popular in Israel, with dishes such as falafel, hummus, and shakshuka.

Israel is also known for its religious diversity. The country is home to a variety of religious communities, including Jews,

Christians, Muslims, and Druze. The city of Jerusalem is particularly significant for its religious importance, as it is home to the Western Wall, the Dome of the Rock, and the Church of the Holy Sepulchre, among other important religious sites.

In addition to its religious and cultural diversity, Israel is also known for its contributions to science and technology. The country has a strong startup culture, and is home to a number of successful technology companies. Israel is also a leader in areas such as water management, renewable energy, and cybersecurity.

In conclusion, Israel is a country with a rich history and culture. Its history spans thousands of years and encompasses a diverse range of peoples and cultures. Its culture is a blend of the many immigrant groups that make up its population, and is characterized by a strong emphasis on education and the arts. Israel is also known for its religious diversity, and its contributions to science and technology. It is a fascinating destination that offers something for everyone.

Geography and Climate

Israel is a small country located in the Middle East, bordered by Lebanon to the north, Syria to the northeast, Jordan to the east, Egypt to the southwest, and the Mediterranean Sea to the west. The country is divided into three main regions: the coastal plain, the hill region, and the desert.

The coastal plain is a narrow strip of land that stretches along the Mediterranean Sea. It is characterized by sandy beaches, dunes, and wetlands. The coastal plain is home to the majority of Israel's population and is the country's economic and cultural center. The major cities in this region include Tel Aviv and Haifa.

The hill region is located in the central part of Israel and is characterized by rolling hills and valleys. It is home to many of Israel's historic sites, including Jerusalem, Hebron, and Bethlehem. The hill region is also home to many of Israel's agricultural communities, and is known for its vineyards and olive groves.

The desert region is located in the southern part of Israel and covers about 60% of the country's land area. It is characterized by rocky terrain, dry riverbeds, and rugged mountains. The desert region is home to a variety of wildlife, including ibex, hyrax, and leopards. The major cities in this region include Beersheba and Eilat.

Israel has a Mediterranean climate, characterized by mild winters and hot summers. The coastal plain and the hill region have a moderate climate, with temperatures ranging between 15-30°C (59-86°F) during the summer and 10-20°C (50-68°F) during the winter. The desert region has a more arid climate, with temperatures ranging between 20-40°C

(68-104°F) during the summer and 5-20°C (41-68°F) during the winter.

The country also receives most of its rainfall during the winter months, with the average annual precipitation ranging from 400mm to 800mm. The coastal plain receives the most rainfall, with an average of 800mm per year, while the desert region receives the least, with an average of 200mm per year.

Israel's geography and climate also plays a major role in shaping the country's economy. The Mediterranean climate and ample rainfall in the coastal plain and hill region make it ideal for agriculture, particularly for citrus fruits, vegetables, and grapes. The desert region, on the other hand, is rich in minerals such as potash, phosphates, and bromine, which are important for the country's industrial sector.

The country's location on the Mediterranean coast also makes it an important shipping and trade hub, connecting Europe, Asia and

Africa. The ports of Haifa and Ashdod are major gateways for goods coming into and out of the country.

In conclusion, Israel's geography and climate play a major role in shaping the country's economy and culture. The coastal plain, hill region, and desert region offer a diverse range of landscapes, from sandy beaches and rolling hills to rugged mountains and dry riverbeds. The Mediterranean climate and ample rainfall in certain regions make it ideal for agriculture, while the desert region is rich in minerals. The country's location on the Mediterranean coast also makes it an important shipping and trade hub.

Tips on language, currency, and customs

When traveling to Israel, it is important to be aware of the language, currency, and customs of the country.

The official language of Israel is Hebrew, however, many Israelis also speak English, particularly in tourist areas. While Hebrew is the language of instruction in schools and the language of the government, English is widely spoken and understood, and you will likely be able to communicate with locals in English. It is always helpful to know a few basic Hebrew phrases such as "Shalom" (hello), "Toda" (thank you), and "Efshar" (excuse me) to communicate with locals.

The currency used in Israel is the New Israeli Shekel (ILS). It is important to note that many places in Israel do not accept foreign currency, so it is best to have some shekels on hand. Credit cards are widely accepted at most hotels, restaurants, and tourist sites. It's also a good idea to have cash on hand for street vendors, street performers, and other small businesses.

When it comes to customs and etiquette, it is important to be aware of the religious and cultural significance of certain places and actions in Israel. For example, it is important to be respectful when visiting religious sites, such as the Western Wall or the Church of the Holy Sepulchre, and to dress modestly. It's also important to be aware of the significance of the Shabbat (the Jewish Sabbath) and to be respectful of those who observe it.

Another important aspect to consider is the ongoing Israeli-Palestinian conflict. It is best to avoid discussing politics or making any political statements while in Israel, as it can be a sensitive topic for many locals.

It's also important to be aware of the different customs and etiquette when it comes to dining in Israel. For example, it is customary to wait for the host to start eating before beginning to eat. And, it's also important to know that it is customary to leave a small amount of food on one's plate at the end of a meal as a sign of respect for the host's generosity.

In conclusion, when traveling to Israel, it's important to be aware of the language, currency, and customs of the country. Knowing a few basic Hebrew phrases, having some shekels on hand, and being respectful of religious and cultural customs can help make your trip more enjoyable. It's also important to be mindful of the ongoing Israeli-Palestinian conflict and to avoid discussing politics while in the country. It's also important to be aware of the customs and etiquette when it comes to dining and to be respectful of the host's generosity.

Chapter 2:   Accommodations:

When it comes to accommodations in Israel, there is a wide range of options available to suit different budgets and preferences. From luxury hotels and resorts to budget-friendly hostels and apartments, there is something for everyone in Israel.

Luxury Hotels: Israel is home to a number of luxury hotels and resorts that offer top-notch amenities and services. These hotels are typically located in major cities such as Tel Aviv, Jerusalem, and Eilat, and offer a range of amenities such as fitness centers, spas, and swimming pools. Many of these hotels also offer stunning views of the Mediterranean Sea or the desert landscape.

Boutique Hotels: For those looking for a more unique and intimate experience, Israel offers a number of boutique hotels. These hotels are typically smaller in size and offer a more personalized service. Many of these hotels are located in charming, historic buildings and offer a unique style and character.

Bed and Breakfasts: For a more homely and intimate experience, many visitors opt for Bed and Breakfasts. These accommodations typically offer a private room and a shared living area, as well as a delicious homemade breakfast. They are a great option for those looking to experience the local culture and meet other travelers.

Hostels: Israel also offers a range of hostels that are a budget-friendly option for backpackers and budget travelers. These accommodations typically offer dormitory-style rooms, shared bathrooms and kitchens, and a common area. They are a great option for those on a tight budget and looking to meet other budget-minded travelers.

Vacation Rentals: Another option for accommodations in Israel is vacation rentals, such as apartments and villas. These rentals are a great option for those looking for a more independent and self-sufficient experience. Many vacation rentals come equipped with a kitchen, living room, and private bathrooms, and offer more space and privacy than a hotel or hostel.

Campsites: For those looking for a more adventurous and outdoor experience, Israel offers a number of campsites. These accommodations are typically located in scenic areas such as national parks and nature reserves and offer amenities such as bathrooms, showers, and outdoor kitchens.

In conclusion, Israel offers a wide range of accommodations to suit different budgets and preferences. From luxury hotels and resorts to budget-friendly hostels and apartments, there is something for everyone in Israel. Whether you're looking for a luxurious experience, a unique and intimate experience, a budget-friendly option, or a more independent and self-sufficient experience, Israel has something to offer everyone. It's important to do your research and plan ahead to ensure that you find the perfect accommodation for your trip.

Options for hotels, hostels, guesthouses, and rental properties in Israel

When it comes to finding the right accommodation in Israel, there are a wide range of options available, including hotels, hostels, guesthouses, and rental properties. Each option has its own unique features and benefits, and it's important to consider your budget, location, and travel style when making a decision.

Hotels:

Hotels in Israel range from luxury resorts to budget-friendly options. Luxury hotels

typically offer amenities such as swimming pools, fitness centers, and spas, and are often located in major cities like Tel Aviv, Jerusalem, and Eilat. Many of these hotels also offer stunning views of the Mediterranean Sea or the desert landscape. Budget-friendly hotels are also available in major cities and tourist destinations. They may not have as many amenities as luxury hotels but offer comfortable stay for a reasonable price.

Hostels:

Hostels in Israel offer budget-friendly accommodation for backpackers and budget travelers. They typically offer dormitory-style rooms, shared bathrooms, and kitchens, and a common area. Hostels are a great option for those on a tight budget and looking to meet other budget-minded travelers. Many hostels also offer private rooms for those who prefer more privacy.

Guesthouses:

Guesthouses in Israel offer a more homely and intimate experience. They typically offer a private room and a shared living area, as well as a delicious homemade breakfast. Guesthouses are a great option for those looking to experience the local culture and meet other travelers. Many guesthouses are located in charming, historic buildings and offer a unique style and character.

Rental Properties:

Rental properties such as apartments and villas are a great option for those looking for a more independent and self-sufficient experience. Many rental properties come equipped with a kitchen, living room, and private bathrooms, and offer more space and privacy than a hotel or hostel. Rental properties can also be a cost-effective option for longer stays or for groups of people traveling together.

Vacation Rentals:

Vacation rentals are a great option for those who want more space and privacy than a hotel or hostel can offer. These rentals can be an apartment, a villa or a house, and come equipped with amenities such as a kitchen, living room, and private bathrooms. Vacation rentals are a great option for families or groups of friends traveling together, as they offer more space and privacy than traditional hotel rooms.

In conclusion, when looking for accommodation in Israel, there are a wide range of options available, including hotels, hostels, guesthouses, rental properties, and vacation rentals. Each option has its own unique features and benefits, and it's important to consider your budget, location, and travel style when making a decision. It's important to do your research and plan ahead to ensure that you find the perfect accommodation for your trip.

Recommendations for budget, mid-range, and luxury accommodations in different parts of the country

When planning a trip to Israel, it's important to consider your budget and what type of accommodation you're looking for. Whether you're looking for budget-friendly options, mid-range options, or luxury accommodations, there are plenty of options available in different parts of the country.

Budget Accommodations:

For those on a budget, there are plenty of budget-friendly options available in Israel. In Tel Aviv, the Abraham Hostel is a popular choice for backpackers and budget travelers. This hostel offers dormitory-style rooms, as well as private rooms, and a shared kitchen and common area. Another budget-friendly option in Tel Aviv is the TLV 88 Hostel, which offers dormitory-style rooms and private rooms, as well as a shared kitchen and common area.

In Jerusalem, the Abraham Hostel Jerusalem is a popular choice for budget travelers. This hostel offers dormitory-style rooms and private rooms, as well as a shared kitchen and common area. Another budget-friendly option in Jerusalem is the Jerusalem Hostel, which offers dormitory-style rooms and private rooms, as well as a shared kitchen and common area.

Mid-Range Accommodations:

For those looking for mid-range options, there are plenty of options available in different parts of the country. In Tel Aviv, the Dan Panorama Tel Aviv is a popular choice. This hotel offers comfortable rooms and amenities such as a fitness center and a swimming pool. Another mid-range option in Tel Aviv is the Hotel Montefiore, which offers comfortable rooms and amenities such as a rooftop terrace and a fitness center.

In Jerusalem, the Inbal Jerusalem Hotel is a popular mid-range option. This hotel offers comfortable rooms and amenities such as a fitness center and a swimming pool. Another mid-range option in Jerusalem is the David Citadel Hotel, which offers comfortable rooms and amenities such as a fitness center and a swimming pool.

Luxury Accommodations:

For those looking for luxury accommodations, there are plenty of options available in different parts of the country. In Tel Aviv, the Royal Beach Tel Aviv is a popular luxury option. This hotel offers luxurious rooms and amenities such as a spa, a fitness center, and a swimming pool. Another luxury option in Tel Aviv is the Dan Tel Aviv, which offers luxurious rooms and amenities such as a spa, a fitness center, and a swimming pool.

In Jerusalem, the King David Jerusalem is a popular luxury option. This hotel offers luxurious rooms and amenities such as a spa, a fitness center, and a swimming pool. Another luxury option in Jerusalem is the Waldorf Astoria Jerusalem, which offers luxurious rooms and amenities such as a spa, a fitness center, and a swimming pool.

In the desert region, the Mitzpe Ramon Guest House is a popular luxury option. This guesthouse offers luxurious rooms and amenities such as a spa, a fitness center, and a swimming pool. Another luxury option in the desert region is the Beresheet hotel, which offers luxurious rooms and amenities such as a spa, a fitness center, and a swimming pool.

In conclusion, there are a wide range of accommodation options available in Israel to suit different budgets, from budget-friendly hostels to luxury hotels. It's important to consider your budget, location, and travel style when making a decision. For budget travelers, Tel Aviv and Jerusalem offer many budget-friendly hostels to choose from. Mid-range travelers have many options such as hotels or guesthouses with basic amenities and comfortable rooms. And for luxury travelers, there are many luxury hotels and resorts in Tel Aviv, Jerusalem, and desert regions with top-notch amenities and services. It's also worth noting that vacation rentals can be a cost-effective option for longer stays or for groups of people traveling together.

Information on amenities and services offered by each type of accommodation

When planning a trip to Israel, it's important to consider the amenities and services offered by the different types of accommodations available. Each type of accommodation offers its own unique set of amenities and services, and it's important to consider your needs and preferences when making a decision.

Hotels:

Hotels in Israel offer a wide range of amenities and services. Luxury hotels typically offer amenities such as swimming pools, fitness centers, and spas. They also offer room service, concierge service, and laundry service. Some luxury hotels also offer business centers, conference rooms, and meeting spaces. Many hotels in Israel also have on-site restaurants and bars, offering a variety of dining options for guests. Budget-friendly hotels may not have as many amenities as luxury hotels but usually have basic amenities such as air conditioning, private bathroom and comfortable bedding.

Hostels:

Hostels in Israel typically offer dormitory-style rooms, shared bathrooms, and kitchens, and a common area. Some hostels also offer private rooms for those who prefer more privacy. Many hostels also offer Wi-Fi, laundry facilities, and a common area with a television. Some hostels also offer a small library or a games room for guests to enjoy. Some hostels also offer a tour desk, where guests can book tours and excursions.

Guesthouses:

Guesthouses in Israel typically offer a private room and a shared living area, as well as a delicious homemade breakfast. They also offer amenities such as air conditioning and private bathrooms. Many guesthouses also offer Wi-Fi, laundry facilities, and a common area with a television. Some guesthouses also offer a small library or a games room for guests to enjoy. Some guesthouses also offer a tour desk, where guests can book tours and excursions.

Rental Properties:

Rental properties such as apartments and villas offer more space and privacy than a hotel or hostel can offer. Many rental properties come equipped with amenities such as a kitchen, living room, and private bathrooms. They also offer amenities such as air conditioning, Wi-Fi, and laundry facilities. Some rental properties also have outdoor spaces such as terraces or gardens, which can be a great option for those looking to enjoy the outdoors during their stay. Many rental properties also offer additional services such as daily housekeeping or concierge services, depending on the property. Vacation rentals offer more flexibility and freedom as guests can cook their own meals and have their own space.

In conclusion, when planning a trip to Israel, it's important to consider the amenities and services offered by the different types of accommodations available. Hotels in Israel offer a wide range of amenities and services, from luxury hotels with top-notch amenities to budget-friendly hotels with basic amenities.

Hostels, guesthouses and rental properties have also their own unique amenities and services, from shared facilities to private spaces, from breakfast to full kitchen. It's important to consider your needs and preferences when making a decision, and also to research and plan ahead to ensure that you find the perfect accommodation for your trip.

Chapter 3:   Transportation

Transportation in Israel is diverse and well-developed, making it easy to get around the country. From buses and trains to taxis and rental cars, there are many options to choose from, depending on your budget and travel needs.

Buses:

Buses are a popular and convenient option for getting around Israel. The bus system is extensive and covers most major cities and tourist destinations. The Egged Bus Cooperative is the main bus company in Israel and operates most of the bus routes. The buses are clean, air-conditioned, and offer a convenient and affordable way to get around. The bus system also offers special bus lines for tourists that cover most of the main attractions in the country. They can be payed with cash, card or by using a "Rav Kav" card.

Trains:

Trains are another popular option for getting around Israel. The Israel Railways operates trains that connect most major cities and tourist destinations. The trains are clean, air-conditioned, and offer a convenient and affordable way to get around. The trains also offer a comfortable and scenic way to travel, as they pass through some of the most beautiful parts of the country.

Taxis:

Taxis are a convenient option for getting around Israel, particularly in the larger cities. Taxis are widely available and can be hailed on the street or booked in advance. It's a good idea to agree on the fare before starting the journey, or to use a taxi-hailing app such as Gett, Careem or Uber. Taxis in Israel are relatively affordable, and most accept credit cards.

Rental Cars:

Rental cars are a popular option for those who prefer to explore the country at their own pace. There are many car rental companies available in Israel, and cars can be rented at airports, train stations, and major cities. It's important to be aware that driving in Israel can be challenging, particularly in the larger cities, where traffic can be heavy and fast-paced. It's also important to be aware of the road rules and regulations, as well as the parking laws.

Bicycles:

Bicycles are a popular option for those who want to explore the country at a slower pace. There are many bicycle rental shops available in Israel, and bicycles can be rented by the hour or by the day. Many cities also offer bike-sharing programs, which can be a convenient option for those who don't want to commit to a full-day rental.

In conclusion, Israel offers a wide range of transportation options, including buses, trains, taxis, rental cars, and bicycles. Each option has its own unique features and benefits, and it's important to consider your budget and travel needs when making a decision. The bus and train system are extensive, affordable and convenient, while taxis and rental cars offer more flexibility. Bicycles are a great option for those who want to explore the country at a slower pace, and bike-sharing programs are available in many cities. It's important to be aware of the road rules and regulations, as well as parking laws, when driving or renting a car in Israel.

Options for getting around Israel , including public transportation, taxis, rental cars, and tours

Getting around Israel is relatively easy and convenient, with a variety of options available including public transportation, taxis, rental cars, and tours. Each option has its own unique features and benefits, and it's important to consider your budget, travel needs, and personal preferences when making a decision.

Public Transportation:

The public transportation system in Israel is well-developed and extensive, with buses and trains connecting most major cities and tourist destinations. The Egged Bus Cooperative is the main bus company in Israel and operates most of the bus routes. Buses are clean, air-conditioned, and offer a convenient and affordable way to get around. The bus system also offers special bus lines for tourists that cover most of the main attractions in the country. The Israel Railways operates trains that connect most major cities and tourist destinations. Trains are clean, air-conditioned, and offer a comfortable and scenic way to travel.

Taxis:

Taxis are a convenient option for getting around Israel, particularly in the larger cities. Taxis are widely available and can be hailed on the street or booked in advance. It's a good idea to agree on the fare before starting the journey, or to use a taxi-hailing app such as Gett, Careem or Uber. Taxis in Israel are relatively affordable, and most accept credit cards.

Rental Cars:

Rental cars are a popular option for those who prefer to explore the country at their own pace. There are many car rental companies available in Israel, and cars can be rented at airports, train stations, and major cities. It's important to be aware that driving in Israel can be challenging, particularly in the larger cities, where traffic can be heavy and fast-paced. It's also important to be aware of the road rules and regulations, as well as the parking laws.

Tours:

Tours are a great option for those who want to see the main attractions in Israel but don't want to navigate the public transportation system or rent a car. There are a wide variety of tours available, including guided bus tours, walking tours, and bike tours. Many tours also include entrance fees to popular attractions and meals. It's important to do research and find a reputable tour company that offers the type of tour that interests you.

Walking:

Walking is a great way to explore many of Israel's cities and neighborhoods, especially in the Old City of Jerusalem, and in the ancient cities of Jaffa, Caesarea, and Acre.

Many of these areas have narrow, winding streets and alleys that are best explored on foot. Walking is also a good way to experience the local culture, as you can take your time and enjoy the sights, sounds, and smells of the city. It's also a great way to save money and get some exercise while exploring.

Ridesharing:

Ridesharing services such as Uber and Gett are available in most major cities in Israel and are a convenient option for getting around. These services can be accessed through a smartphone app and allow users to quickly and easily book a ride. They are generally more affordable than traditional taxis and can be a good option for those who are comfortable with using technology.

In conclusion, there are many options for getting around Israel, including public transportation, taxis, rental cars, tours, walking and ridesharing. Each option has its own unique features and benefits, and it's important to consider your budget, travel needs, and personal preferences when making a decision. The public transportation system is extensive and affordable, while taxis and rental cars offer more flexibility. Tours are a great option for those who want to see the main attractions, walking is a great way to explore the cities and neighborhoods and ridesharing services are a convenient option for those who are comfortable with using technology.

Chapter 4:   Food and Drink:

The food and drink scene in Israel is diverse and delicious, with a mix of traditional and modern dishes influenced by the country's diverse population. From falafel and shawarma to hummus and shakshuka, there are plenty of options to choose from.

Traditional Israeli Cuisine:

Traditional Israeli cuisine is heavily influenced by the country's Middle Eastern and Mediterranean roots. Some of the most popular traditional dishes include falafel, shawarma, hummus, and shakshuka. Falafel is a deep-fried ball or patty made from ground chickpeas or fava beans, often served in a pita with various toppings such as tahini and vegetables. Shawarma is a dish of meat cooked on a spit and shaved off for serving, typically served in a pita with various toppings such as tahini and vegetables. Hummus is a dip or spread made from chickpeas, tahini, lemon juice, and garlic, often served as an appetizer with pita bread. Shakshuka is a dish of eggs poached in a flavorful tomato sauce with spices and vegetables, often served with bread for dipping.

Middle Eastern Cuisine:

Middle Eastern cuisine is also popular in Israel, with dishes such as kebab, kofta, and kubbeh being a staple. Kebab is a dish of meat cooked on a skewer, often served with rice or in a pita. Kofta is a dish of ground meat, usually beef or lamb, mixed with spices and formed into balls or cylinders, often served with a side of rice or vegetables. Kubbeh is a dish made from ground meat and bulgur wheat, shaped into balls and then fried or cooked in a soup.

Seafood:

Israel has a Mediterranean coastline, and seafood is a staple in the diet of the country. Some popular seafood dishes include fish shawarma, fish and chips, and seafood platters. Fish shawarma is a variation of the traditional shawarma but made with fish instead of meat. Fish and chips is a popular dish that can be found in almost every seafood restaurant, it's a deep-fried fish fillet served with french fries and tartar sauce. Seafood platters are also a popular option, and typically include a variety of seafood such as fish, squid, and shrimp, often served with a side of vegetables or salad.

Desserts:

Israeli cuisine has a wide variety of desserts, and the most popular include baklava, halva, and knafeh. Baklava is a sweet pastry made from layers of phyllo dough and honey or syrup, often filled with nuts or seeds. Halva is a sweet confection made from sesame paste and sugar, often flavored with fruits or nuts. Knafeh is a sweet pastry made from phyllo dough and cheese, often served with a sweet syrup.

Drinks:

Israel is home to a variety of traditional and modern drinks, from classic Middle Eastern teas to contemporary cocktails. Arak is a traditional Middle Eastern anise-flavored liquor, often served with water and ice. Israeli wine is also popular, with many wineries located throughout the country producing a variety of red, white, and rosé wines. Israeli beer is also popular and can be found in most bars and restaurants.

In conclusion, the food and drink scene in Israel is diverse and delicious, with a mix of traditional and modern dishes influenced by the country's diverse population. From falafel and shawarma to hummus and shakshuka, there are plenty of options to choose from. Middle Eastern cuisine is also popular with The food and drink scene in Israel is diverse and delicious, with a mix of traditional and modern dishes influenced by the country's diverse population. From falafel and shawarma to hummus and shakshuka, there are plenty of options to choose from.

Traditional Israeli Cuisine:

Traditional Israeli cuisine is heavily influenced by the country's Middle Eastern and Mediterranean roots. Some of the most popular traditional dishes include falafel, shawarma, hummus, and shakshuka. Falafel is a deep-fried ball or patty made from ground chickpeas or fava beans, often served in a pita with various toppings such as tahini and vegetables. Shawarma is a dish of meat cooked on a spit and shaved off for serving, typically served in a pita with various toppings such as tahini and vegetables. Hummus is a dip or spread made from chickpeas, tahini, lemon juice, and garlic, often served as an appetizer with pita bread. Shakshuka is a dish of eggs poached in a flavorful tomato sauce with spices and vegetables, often served with bread for dipping.

Middle Eastern Cuisine:

Middle Eastern cuisine is also popular in Israel, with dishes such as kebab, kofta, and kubbeh being a staple. Kebab is a dish of meat cooked on a skewer, often served with rice or in a pita. Kofta is a dish of ground meat, usually beef or lamb, mixed with spices and formed into balls or cylinders, often served with a side of rice or vegetables. Kubbeh is a dish made from ground meat and bulgur wheat, shaped into balls and then fried or cooked in a soup.

Seafood:

Israel has a Mediterranean coastline, and seafood is a staple in the diet of the country. Some popular seafood dishes include fish shawarma, fish and chips, and seafood platters. Fish shawarma is a variation of the traditional shawarma but made with fish instead of meat. Fish and chips is a popular dish that can be found in almost every seafood restaurant, it's a deep-fried fish fillet served with french fries and tartar sauce. Seafood platters are also a popular option, and typically include a variety of seafood such as fish, squid, and shrimp, often served with a side of vegetables or salad.

Desserts:

Israeli cuisine has a wide variety of desserts, and the most popular include baklava, halva, and knafeh. Baklava is a sweet pastry made from layers of phyllo dough and honey or syrup, often filled with nuts or seeds. Halva is a sweet confection made from sesame paste and sugar, often flavored with fruits or nuts. Knafeh is a sweet pastry made from phyllo dough and cheese, often served with a sweet syrup.

Drinks:

Israel is home to a variety of traditional and modern drinks, from classic Middle Eastern teas to contemporary cocktails. Arak is a traditional Middle Eastern anise-flavored liquor, often served with water and ice. Israeli wine is also popular, with many wineries located throughout the country producing a variety of red, white, and rosé wines. Israeli beer is also popular and can be found in most bars and restaurants.

In conclusion, the food and drink scene in Israel is diverse and delicious, with a mix of traditional and modern dishes influenced by the country's diverse population. From falafel and shawarma to hummus and shakshuka, there are plenty of options to choose from. Middle Eastern cuisine is also popular with dishes such as kebab, kofta, and kubbeh being a staple. Israel's Mediterranean coastline also makes seafood a staple in the diet of the country. Desserts and traditional drinks like Arak are also popular and can be found in most restaurants. The country has a burgeoning wine industry with many wineries producing a variety of red, white, and rosé wines. Israeli beer is also a popular option and can be found in most bars and restaurants.

There are many options for food and drink in Israel, and it's a great opportunity to experience the diverse and delicious culinary scene that the country has to offer.

Overview of Israel cuisine and dining options, including recommended restaurants and local specialties

Israel cuisine is a melting pot of flavors and cultures, reflecting the country's diverse population. The cuisine is heavily influenced by the Middle Eastern and Mediterranean regions, and is known for its fresh ingredients, bold spices, and healthy options. The country's diverse dining scene offers a wide range of options, from street food to fine dining, and there's something for every taste and budget.

Traditional Israeli Cuisine:

Traditional Israeli cuisine is heavily influenced by the country's Middle Eastern and Mediterranean roots. Some of the most popular traditional dishes include falafel, shawarma, hummus, and shakshuka. Falafel is a deep-fried ball or patty made from ground chickpeas or fava beans, often served in a pita with various toppings such as tahini and vegetables. Shawarma is a dish of meat cooked on a spit and shaved off for serving, typically served in a pita with various toppings such as tahini and vegetables. Hummus is a dip or spread made from chickpeas, tahini, lemon juice, and garlic, often served as an appetizer with pita bread. Shakshuka is a dish of eggs poached in a flavorful tomato sauce with spices and vegetables, often served with bread for dipping.

Middle Eastern Cuisine:

Middle Eastern cuisine is also popular in Israel, with dishes such as kebab, kofta, and kubbeh being a staple. Kebab is a dish of meat cooked on a skewer, often served with rice or in a pita. Kofta is a dish of ground meat, usually beef or lamb, mixed with spices and formed into balls or cylinders, often served with a side of rice or vegetables. Kubbeh is a dish made from ground meat and bul gur wheat, shaped into balls and then fried or cooked in a soup. Some popular restaurants that serve traditional Middle Eastern cuisine include Abu Hassan in Jaffa, which is known for its delicious hummus, and Ta'ami in Jerusalem, which is famous for its shawarma.

Seafood:

Israel's Mediterranean coastline makes seafood a staple in the country's diet, and there are many seafood restaurants located throughout the country. Some popular seafood dishes include fish shawarma, fish and chips, and seafood platters. Fish shawarma is a variation of the traditional shawarma but made with fish instead of meat. Fish and chips is a popular dish that can be found in almost every seafood restaurant, it's a deep-fried fish fillet served with french fries and tartar sauce. Seafood platters are also a popular option, and typically include a variety of seafood such as fish, squid, and shrimp, often served with a side of vegetables or salad. Some recommended seafood restaurants include the Port in Tel Aviv, which offers a variety of fresh seafood dishes and has a beautiful seaside location, and the Fish Market in Haifa, which serves fresh and delicious seafood in a casual and lively atmosphere.

Fine Dining:

Israel's dining scene also offers a variety of fine dining options, with many restaurants featuring innovative and creative cuisine. Some popular fine dining restaurants include Shila in Tel Aviv, which serves contemporary Middle Eastern cuisine and has been awarded a Michelin star, and M25 in Jerusalem, which offers a unique fusion of Mediterranean and Asian flavors.

Street Food:

For a more casual and affordable dining experience, Israel's street food scene is worth exploring. Some popular street foods include falafel, shawarma, and sabich, which is a sandwich made with fried eggplant, boiled egg, and various toppings. Some recommended street food spots include the Falafel stand in Jerusalem's Mahane Yehuda market, which is known for its delicious falafel, and the Shawarma stand in Tel Aviv's Carmel market, which serves mouthwatering shawarma.

In conclusion, Israel's dining scene offers a wide range of options, from street food to fine dining, and there's something for every taste and budget. Traditional Israeli cuisine and Middle Eastern cuisine are popular and delicious, with seafood being a staple due to the country's Mediterranean coastline. Fine dining options are also available for those looking for an upscale dining experience. Street food is also a great option for a more casual and affordable dining experience. There are many restaurants and local specialties to choose from, so it's recommended to do some research and make reservations in advance.

Tips on finding the best food and drink experiences, such as local markets, food tours, and cooking classes

Exploring the local food and drink scene is one of the best ways to experience a new place, and Israel has a rich and diverse culinary culture that is worth discovering. Whether you're looking for traditional dishes, seafood, fine dining, or street food, there are many ways to find the best food and drink experiences in Israel. Here are some tips on finding the best food and drink experiences in Israel:

Local Markets:

Visiting local markets is a great way to experience the local food and drink culture. In Israel, there are many popular markets such as the Mahane Yehuda market in Jerusalem, the Carmel market in Tel Aviv, and the Hadar market in Haifa. These markets offer a wide variety of fresh produce, meat, seafood, and spices, as well as street food and local specialties. They are also great places to meet locals and learn about the local culture.

Food Tours:

Food tours are a great way to explore the local food and drink scene while learning about the history and culture. Many tour companies offer food tours in Israel, which take you to popular street food stands, local markets, and traditional restaurants. These tours often include tastings of local specialties, and can be a great way to get an overview of the local cuisine.

Cooking Classes:

Cooking classes are a great way to learn about the local food and drink culture, and to take home a new skill. Many cooking schools in Israel offer classes that focus on traditional Israeli and Middle Eastern cuisine, and some classes even include trips to local markets to buy ingredients. These classes often include hands-on instruction, and can be a great way to learn about the local cuisine and culture.

Food Blogs and Social Media:

Following food bloggers and social media influencers in Israel can be a great way to discover new places to eat and drink, and to learn about local food and drink culture. Many food bloggers and social media influencers in Israel share their favorite restaurants, local markets, and street food stands, and can give you great recommendations for where to eat and drink.

Ask the locals:

Asking locals for recommendations is a great way to discover new places to eat and drink, and to learn about the local food and drink culture. Many locals in Israel are happy to share their favorite restaurants, local markets, and street food stands, and can give you great recommendations for where to eat and drink.

In conclusion, exploring the local food and drink scene is one of the best ways to experience a new place, and Israel has a rich and diverse culinary culture that is worth discovering. Visiting local markets, taking food tours, and taking cooking classes are great ways to learn about the local cuisine and culture. Following food bloggers and social media influencers, and asking locals for recommendations can also give you great tips on where to find the best food and drink experiences in Israel.

Chapter 5: Activities and Attractions:

Israel is a country with a rich history and culture, and there are many activities and attractions to explore. Whether you're interested in history, religion, nature, or adventure, there's something for everyone. Here are some popular activities and attractions to consider when visiting Israel:

Historical and Religious Sites:

Israel is home to many historical and religious sites, including the Western Wall and the Dome of the Rock in Jerusalem, which are considered to be the holiest site in Judaism, and the Church of the Holy Sepulchre, which is considered to be one of the holiest sites in Christianity. Other historical and religious sites include the ancient city of Caesarea, which was built by King Herod, and the ancient city of Acre, which was a major port during the Crusades.

Nature and Adventure:

Israel is home to many natural and adventure activities, including hiking and camping in the Golan Heights, snorkeling and diving in the Red Sea, and bird-watching in the Hula Valley. The country has also many National Parks such as Ein Gedi, Masada and the Dead Sea which are popular for hiking, swimming, and experiencing the unique and beautiful landscape.

Beaches:

Israel's Mediterranean coastline offers some of the best beaches in the region, with many beaches offering excellent swimming and sunbathing opportunities. Some popular beaches include the beaches of Tel Aviv, which are known for their lively atmosphere and nightlife, and the beaches of Eilat, which are known for their crystal-clear waters and vibrant coral reefs.

Shopping:

Israel offers a wide range of shopping options, from traditional souks and markets to modern malls and designer boutiques. Some popular shopping destinations include the Carmel market in Tel Aviv, which is known for its variety of fresh produce, spices, and street food, and the Jaffa Flea Market in Jaffa, which is known for its antiques, vintage clothing, and crafts.

Museums:

Israel is home to many museums, including the Israel Museum in Jerusalem, which is known for its collection of Jewish and Israeli art and artifacts, and the Tel Aviv Museum of Art, which is known for its collection of contemporary art. Other popular museums include the Holocaust Memorial Museum in Jerusalem, and the Museum of the History of Tel Aviv-Yafo, which provides a glimpse into the history and culture of the city.

In conclusion, Israel is a country with a rich history and culture, and there are many activities and attractions to explore. Whether you're interested in history, religion, nature, or adventure, there's something for everyone. Historical and religious sites, nature and adventure activities, beaches, shopping, and museums are some of the popular activities and attractions to consider when visiting Israel. It's a great opportunity to discover the country's rich culture and history, and to experience the unique and beautiful landscape.

Overview of the top things to do and see in Israel , including museums, landmarks, outdoor activities, and cultural experiences

Israel is a country that has a rich history, culture, and natural beauty, and there are many top things to do and see. Whether you're interested in history, religion, nature, or culture, there's something for everyone. Here's an overview of the top things to do and see in Israel:

Historical and Religious Sites:

Israel is home to many historical and religious sites, including the Western Wall and the Dome of the Rock in Jerusalem, which are considered to be the holiest site in Judaism, and the Church of the Holy Sepulchre, which is considered to be one of the holiest sites in Christianity. Other historical and religious sites include the ancient city of Caesarea, which was built by King Herod, the ancient city of Acre, which was a major port during the Crusades, and the ancient city of Masada, which is a UNESCO World Heritage Site and a symbol of Jewish resistance during the Roman period.

Museums:

Israel is home to many museums, including the Israel Museum in Jerusalem, which is known for its collection of Jewish and Israeli art and artifacts, and the Tel Aviv Museum of Art, which is known for its collection of contemporary art. Other popular museums include the Holocaust Memorial Museum in Jerusalem, which is dedicated to remembering the victims of the Holocaust, and the Museum of the History of Tel Aviv-Yafo, which provides a glimpse into the history and culture of the city.

Outdoor Activities:

Israel offers many outdoor activities for nature lovers, such as hiking and camping in the Golan Heights, snorkeling and diving in the Red Sea, and bird-watching in the Hula Valley. The country has also many National Parks such as Ein Gedi, Masada and the Dead Sea which are popular for hiking, swimming, and experiencing the unique and beautiful landscape. The Dead Sea is one of the most popular tourist destinations in Israel, and is known for its high salt content, which allows for floating and its healing properties. Visitors can also take a dip in the mineral-rich waters, apply the mud on their skin, and enjoy the beautiful surrounding landscapes.

Cultural Experiences:

Israel offers a wide range of cultural experiences, from visiting traditional souks and markets, to experiencing the country's vibrant nightlife and music scene. Some popular cultural experiences include visiting the Old City of Jerusalem, which is home to many historical and religious sites, and the Carmel market in Tel Aviv, which is known for its variety of fresh produce, spices, and street food. Visitors can also enjoy the local cuisine and try traditional dishes such as falafel, shawarma, and hummus.

In conclusion, Israel is a country that has a rich history, culture, and natural beauty, and there are many top things to do and see. Historical and religious sites, museums, outdoor activities, and cultural experiences are some of the top things to do and see in Israel. The country offers a wide range of options for visitors, from exploring ancient cities, visiting holy sites, and experiencing the unique and beautiful landscapes, to learning about the country's history and culture, and sampling the delicious local cuisine. It's a great opportunity to discover the country's rich culture and history, and to experience the unique and beautiful landscape.

Tips on finding the best activities and attractions, such as guided tours and off-the-beaten-path experiences

Israel is a country with a rich history, culture and natural beauty and there are many activities and attractions to explore. With so much to see and do, it can be overwhelming to plan your itinerary. Here are some tips on finding the best activities and attractions, such as guided tours and off-the-beaten-path experiences:

Guided Tours:

Guided tours are a great way to explore the country and to learn more about its history and culture. Many tour companies offer guided tours in Israel, which can take you to the most popular historical and religious sites, such as the Western Wall, the Dome of the Rock, and the Church of the Holy Sepulchre. Guided tours can also take you to the popular natural and adventure activities, such as hiking and camping in the Golan Heights and snorkeling and diving in the Red Sea. They can also take you to the most popular museums and art galleries.

Off-the-Beatath Experiences:

While the popular tourist destinations in Israel are definitely worth a visit, there are also many off-the-beaten-path experiences to be had. These can include visiting lesser-known historical sites, such as the ancient city of Beit She'an, or taking a hike in the little-visited nature reserves such as the Jerusalem Hills. Exploring small, charming neighborhoods in cities such as Tel Aviv and Jerusalem, and taking a trip to the smaller towns such as Tiberias and Safed to get a glimpse of local life and culture can also be an enriching experience.

Research before you go:

It's important to research and plan your trip before you go to make the most of your time in Israel. This can include researching the best time to visit, what to pack, and what to expect. It's also a good idea to research the different regions of Israel and decide which areas you want to visit, as each region has its own unique culture, history, and attractions. This research can also help you to identify off-the-beaten-path experiences, such as local markets and hidden gems, that you may not have known about otherwise.

Local Recommendations:

Asking locals for recommendations is a great way to discover new activities and attractions, and to learn about the country's culture and history. Many locals in Israel are happy to share their favorite historical sites, natural attractions, and cultural experiences, and can give you great tips on where to find the best activities and attractions.

Travel Blogs and Social Media:

Following travel bloggers and social media influencers in Israel can also be a great way to discover new activities and attractions. Many travel bloggers and social media influencers in Israel share their experiences and recommendations, and can give you great tips on where to find the best activities and attractions, as well as off-the-beaten-path experiences.

In conclusion, Israel is a country with a rich history, culture and natural beauty, and there are many activities and attractions to explore. Guided tours, off-the-beaten-path experiences, researching before you go, local recommendations, and following travel blogs and social media influencers are all great ways to find the best activities and attractions in Israel. It's important to research and plan your trip to make the most of your time in the country, and to discover the unique and enriching experiences that Israel has to offer.

Chapter 6: Detailed information on popular tourist destinations, including Jerusalem, Tel Aviv, the Dead Sea, and the Galilee region

Israel is a country with a rich history, culture, and natural beauty, and there are many popular tourist destinations to visit. From the ancient city of Jerusalem, to the modern metropolis of Tel Aviv, to the natural wonders of the Dead Sea and the Galilee region, there's something for everyone. Here's detailed information on some of the most popular tourist destinations in Israel:

Jerusalem:

Jerusalem is the capital and largest city of Israel, and is one of the oldest cities in the world. It is also considered to be one of the holiest cities in the world for Jews, Christians, and Muslims. The city is home to many historical and religious sites, such as the Western Wall and the Dome of the Rock, which are considered to be the holiest site in Judaism, and the Church of the Holy Sepulchre, which is considered to be one of the holiest sites in Christianity. The city is also home to the Israel Museum, which has a large collection of Jewish and Israeli art and artifacts, and the Holocaust Memorial Museum, which is dedicated to remembering the victims of the Holocaust.

Tel Aviv:

Tel Aviv is the second-largest city in Israel, and is known for its vibrant culture, nightlife, and beaches. The city is a major center for art, music, and theater, and is home to many museums, such as the Tel Aviv Museum of Art, which has a large collection of contemporary art. The city also has many beaches, such as the beaches of Tel Aviv, which are known for their lively atmosphere and nightlife. Tel Aviv is also known for its street food, and is home to many popular street food stands and markets, such as the Carmel market.

The Dead Sea:

The Dead Sea is one of the most popular tourist destinations in Israel, and is known for its high salt content, which allows for floating and its healing properties. Visitors can also take a dip in the mineral-rich waters, apply the mud on their skin, and enjoy the beautiful surrounding landscapes. The area is also home to many natural spas and wellness centers, where visitors can enjoy various treatments and therapies.

The Galilee Region:

The Galilee region is located in the northern part of Israel, and is known for its natural beauty and historical and religious sites. The region is home to many nature reserves, such as the Hula Valley, which is known for its bird-watching, and the Golan Heights, which is known for its hiking and camping. The region is also home to many historical and religious sites, such as the ancient city of Tiberias, which is considered to be one of the four holy cities in Judaism, and the Church of the Beatitudes, which is believed to be the site of Jesus' Sermon on the Mount.

In conclusion, Israel is a country with a rich history, culture, and natural beauty, and there are many popular tourist destinations to visit. Jerusalem, Tel Aviv, the Dead Sea, and the Galilee region are some of the most popular tourist destinations in Israel. Each destination offers a unique experience, whether it be exploring ancient historical and religious sites, experiencing the vibrant culture and nightlife, relaxing and rejuvenating in natural spas, or hiking and enjoying the beautiful landscapes. Jerusalem offers an opportunity to delve into the rich history and religious significance of the city. Tel Aviv offers a modern and cosmopolitan experience with its museums, beaches, street food and nightlife. The Dead Sea offers a unique experience of floating in its mineral-rich waters and rejuvenating with the mud and spa treatments. The Galilee region offers a chance to explore the natural beauty of the area and visit historical and religious sites. Each destination offers a unique and enriching experience, and it is recommended to consider visiting multiple destinations to fully experience all that Israel has to offer.

Chapter 7: Special events and festivals

Israel is a country with a rich history, culture, and diverse society, and there are many special events and festivals that take place throughout the year. These events and festivals offer visitors the opportunity to experience the country's culture and traditions, and to enjoy various forms of music, art, food, and entertainment. Here's an overview of some of the most popular special events and festivals in Israel:

Purim:

Purim is a Jewish holiday that celebrates the salvation of the Jewish people from the Persian Empire, as told in the biblical Book of Esther. It is a joyous holiday, celebrated with costumes, parades, and the reading of the Megillah (the Scroll of Esther) in synagogues. The main customs of Purim are sending gifts of food and drink to one another, and giving gifts of money to the poor. In Jerusalem and other cities, people dress up in costumes, and there are parades, street parties, and other celebrations.

Yom Ha'atzmaut:

Yom Ha'atzmaut is Israel's Independence Day, celebrated on the fifth of Iyar, which marks the day that Israel declared its independence in 1948. The day is celebrated with parades, concerts, and other events throughout the country. There are also many street parties and celebrations, where people gather to enjoy food, drink, and music.

Passover:

Passover, or Pesach, is a Jewish holiday that commemorates the liberation of the Israelites from slavery in Egypt, as told in the Bible. It is one of the most widely observed Jewish holidays and is celebrated in the spring. The holiday is marked by the eating of matzah, a type of unleavened bread, and the avoidance of leavened products. Many families gather for a special meal, called a Seder, on the first night of Passover.

Sukkot:

Sukkot is a Jewish holiday that commemorates the time that the Israelites spent in the wilderness after leaving Egypt, as told in the Bible. It is celebrated in the fall, and one of the main customs of Sukkot is to build and dwell in a sukkah, a temporary hut. Many families build sukkahs in their gardens or on their balconies, and decorate them with fruit, leaves, and other natural decorations. Sukkot is also a time for family gatherings, where people share meals and celebrate together.

Rosh Hashanah:

Rosh Hashanah is the Jewish New Year, and is celebrated in the fall. It is a time for reflection and repentance, and is marked by the sounding of the shofar, a ram's horn, in synagogues. Many people attend synagogue services and hear the shofar blown, and families gather for festive meals.

Hanukkah:

Hanukkah is a Jewish holiday that commemorates the miracle of the oil that burned for eight days in the Temple in Jerusalem. It is celebrated in December, and one of the main customs of Hanukkah is to light a menorah, a nine-branched cand holder, with one candle lit each night. Many families also exchange gifts and play with dreidels, a four-sided spinning top.

In conclusion, Israel is a country with a rich history, culture, and diverse society, and there are many special events and festivals that take place throughout the year. Purim, Yom Ha'atzmaut, Passover, Sukkot, Rosh Hashanah, and Hanukkah are some of the most popular special events and festivals in Israel. Each event or festival offers a unique opportunity to experience the country's culture and traditions, and to enjoy various forms of music, art, food, and entertainment. It is recommended to plan your trip to Israel during these events and festivals to experience the country in a different way and immerse yourself in the local culture.

Chapter 8:   Traveling with kids and families

Traveling with kids and families can be a great way to bond and create lasting memories, but it also requires some extra planning and consideration. Israel is a country with many family-friendly activities and attractions, and there are many ways to make your trip fun, educational, and safe for children. Here's some tips on traveling with kids and families in Israel:

Consider the time of year you travel: Israel has a hot and dry climate, so it's best to avoid traveling during the summer months when temperatures can be very high. Spring and fall are the best seasons to visit with milder temperatures and less crowds.

Choose accommodation that suits your family's needs: Many hotels and vacation rentals in Israel offer family-friendly amenities such as connecting rooms, cribs, and children's menus. You may also want to consider staying in a vacation rental with a kitchen and outdoor space, which can provide more flexibility and comfort for families.

Plan age-appropriate activities: Israel has a wide range of activities and attractions that are suitable for families, such as visiting historical and religious sites, taking a dip in the Dead Sea, going on a nature hike, and visiting zoos and aquariums. It's important to plan activities that are age-appropriate for your children, so they can enjoy and learn from the experience.

Pack for your children's needs: Make sure to pack enough clothing and sunscreen for your children, as well as any necessary medications and comfort items. Bring snacks, drinks and activities to keep them occupied during long journeys or quiet moments.

Be aware of safety concerns: Israel is a safe country to visit, but it's important to be aware of potential safety concerns, such as traffic and crowds. Keep a close eye on your children at all times, and make sure they know what to do in case of emergency.

Learn about Israeli culture: Israel is a country with a rich history, culture and diverse society. Take the opportunity to learn about Israeli culture, customs and traditions with your kids. Many museums and historical sites have special activities and programs for kids that can make learning fun and interactive.

Take advantage of guided tours: Guided tours are a great way to explore the country and to learn more about its history and culture. Many tour companies offer guided tours that are suitable for families, which can take you to the most popular historical and religious sites, such as the Western Wall, the Dome of the Rock, and the Church of the Holy Sepulchre.

Be flexible: Traveling with kids and families can sometimes require a more flexible approach. Be prepared for unexpected changes in plans, and have backup options in case things don't go as planned. Remember to take time to relax and enjoy the journey, and don't put too much pressure on yourself to see and do everything.

In conclusion, traveling with kids and families in Israel can be a great way to bond and create lasting memories. It's important to consider the time of year you travel, choose family-friendly accommodation, plan age-appropriate activities, pack for your children's needs, be aware of safety concerns, learn about Israeli culture, take advantage of guided tours, and be flexible. With the right planning and preparation, your family can have a safe, fun, and educational trip to Israel.

Kid-friendly attractions and activities

Israel is a country with a rich history, culture, and natural beauty, and there are many kid-friendly attractions and activities to explore. From historical and religious sites, to natural parks and beaches, to interactive museums and fun activities, there's something for every age and interest. Here's an overview of some of the most popular kid-friendly attractions and activities in Israel:

1. Old City of Jerusalem: The Old City of Jerusalem is a historical and religious site that is perfect for families to explore. The city is home to many historical and religious sites, such as the Western Wall, the Dome of the Rock, and the Church of the Holy Sepulchre. The city also has many fun and interactive activities, such as guided tours, which can make learning about the history and culture of the city fun and engaging for kids.

2. Ein Gedi National Park: This national park is located on the shores of the Dead Sea and is known for its beautiful landscapes and diverse wildlife. The park is a great place for families to hike and explore, and there are many fun and interactive activities, such as guided tours, bird-watching, and swimming in the Dead Sea.

3. Tel Aviv Port: The Tel Aviv Port is a popular destination for families, and is known for its lively atmosphere, restaurants, and entertainment. The port also has many fun and interactive activities, such as a playground, and a water park that can be enjoyed by kids.

4. Science Museum: The Bloomfield Science Museum in Jerusalem is a popular destination for families and is known for its interactive and educational exhibits. The museum has many fun and interactive activities,

such as hands-on experiments and interactive displays, that can make learning about science and technology fun and engaging for kids.

5. The Israel Museum: This Museum in Jerusalem is home to a large collection of Jewish and Israeli art and artifacts, and is a great place for families to explore. The museum has many fun and interactive activities, such as guided tours and workshops, that can make learning about the history and culture of Israel fun and engaging for kids.

6. The Jerusalem Biblical Zoo: This zoo is home to many different species of animals and is a great place for families to explore. The zoo also offers guided tours, interactive exhibits, and animal encounters, which can make learning about animals and conservation fun and engaging for kids.

7. The Dead Sea: The Dead Sea is one of the most popular tourist destinations in Israel, and is known for its mineral-rich waters and healing properties. The Dead Sea is a great place for families to relax and rejuvenate, and there are many kid-friendly activities, such as swimming, mud baths, and spa treatments that can be enjoyed by the whole family.

8. The Carmel Market: The Carmel Market in Tel Aviv is a popular destination for families, and is known for its lively atmosphere, street food, and shopping. The market also has many fun and interactive activities, such as cooking classes, where kids can learn how to make traditional Israeli dishes.

9. Water Parks: Israel has many water parks which can be enjoyed by kids, such as 'Water World' in Ashdod and 'Waves' in Ashkelon. These water

parks have many fun and interactive activities such as water slides, lazy rivers, wave pools, and children's play areas.

10. Playgrounds: Israel has many playgrounds throughout the country, which can be enjoyed by kids, such as the playground in the Independence Park in Jerusalem, and the playground in the Charles Clore Park in Tel Aviv. These playgrounds have many fun and interactive activities such as swings, slides, climbing structures and more.

In conclusion, Israel is a country with many kid-friendly attractions and activities that can be enjoyed by families. From historical and religious sites, to natural parks and beaches, to interactive museums and fun activities, there's something for every age and interest. Some of the most popular kid-friendly attractions and activities in Israel include the Old City of Jerusalem, Ein Gedi

National Park, Tel Aviv Port, Science Museum, The Israel Museum, The Jerusalem Biblical Zoo, The Dead Sea, The Carmel Market, Water Parks and Playgrounds. It is recommended to plan your trip to Israel keeping in mind the interests and age of your children to make the most of your time in the country.

Tips for traveling with children

Traveling with children can be a rewarding and enjoyable experience, but it also requires some extra planning and preparation. Here are some tips for traveling with children in Israel:

1. Involve the children in the planning process: Involve children in the planning process, this will make them more excited about the trip and they will feel like they have a say in what they want to do. Show them pictures and videos of the destinations you

plan to visit, and let them make a list of the things they want to see and do.

2. Pack for your children's needs: Pack enough clothes, sunscreen, hats, and comfortable shoes for your children. Also, bring along any necessary medications, and comfort items such as a favorite toy or blanket. Pack snacks and drinks to keep them energized and hydrated throughout the day.

3. Be prepared for unexpected changes in plans: Traveling with children can be unpredictable, and you should be prepared for unexpected changes in plans. Have a backup plan in case your child gets sick or an attraction is closed.

4. Take advantage of family-friendly accommodations: Many hotels and vacation rentals in Israel offer family-friendly amenities such as connecting rooms, cribs, and children's menus. Consider staying in

a vacation rental with a kitchen and outdoor space, which can provide more flexibility and comfort for families.

5. Plan age-appropriate activities: Israel has a wide range of activities and attractions that are suitable for families, but it's important to plan activities that are age-appropriate for your children. Research the attractions you plan to visit, and look for activities that will be fun and engaging for your children.

6. Be aware of safety concerns: Israel is a safe country to visit, but it's important to be aware of potential safety concerns, such as traffic and crowds. Keep a close eye on your children at all times, and make sure they know what to do in case of emergency.

7. Be flexible: Traveling with children can sometimes require a more flexible approach. Be prepared for unexpected changes in plans, and have backup

options in case things don't go as planned. Remember to take time to relax and enjoy the journey, and don't put too much pressure on yourself to see and do everything. Remember that children are more resilient than we think and can adapt to a change of plans and different environments.

8. Take breaks: Traveling with children can be tiring, both for you and for them. Make sure to take frequent breaks throughout the day, and give them time to rest and recharge. This can include taking a nap, having a snack, or playing at a playground.

9. Learn about Israeli culture: Israel is a country with a rich history, culture, and diverse society. Take the opportunity to learn about Israeli culture, customs, and traditions with your children. Many museums and historical sites have special activities and programs for children that can make learning fun and interactive.

10. Have fun: Last but not least, make sure to have fun! Traveling with children can be a wonderful experience, and it's important to enjoy the journey and make lasting memories with your family.

In conclusion, traveling with children in Israel can be a great way to bond and create lasting memories. It's important to involve children in the planning process, pack for their needs, be prepared for unexpected changes, take advantage of family-friendly accommodations, plan age-appropriate activities, be aware of safety concerns, be flexible, take breaks, learn about Israeli culture, and have fun. With the right planning and preparation, your family can have a safe, fun, and educational trip to Israel.

Chapter 9:   Shopping

Israel is a country with a rich and diverse culture, and it offers a wide range of shopping options for visitors. From traditional markets to modern malls, there is something for everyone. Here are some tips for shopping in Israel:

Visit traditional markets: Israel has a wide range of traditional markets, such as the Carmel Market in Tel Aviv, the Mahane Yehuda Market in Jerusalem, and the Shuk HaCarmel in Haifa. These markets offer a unique shopping experience, and are a great way to immerse yourself in the local culture. You can find a variety of products such as fresh produce, spices, souvenirs, clothing, jewelry, and more.

Look for local and handmade products: Israel is home to many talented artisans and designers, and you can find a wide range of local and handmade products in markets and shops throughout the country. These products include ceramics, textiles, jewelry, and more. Shopping for local and handmade products is a great way to support the local economy and take home a unique and authentic piece of Israel.

Explore the shopping centers: Israel has many modern shopping centers, such as the Azrieli Center in Tel Aviv, and the Malha Mall in Jerusalem. These centers offer a wide range of shops, restaurants, and entertainment options, and are a great place to find international brands and products.

Shop for jewelry: Israel is known for its jewelry and you can find a wide range of high-quality and unique jewelry in shops and markets throughout the country. The most popular types of jewelry are the traditional Jewish jewelry, such as the Hamsa and the Star of David. Israel is also famous for its diamonds, so you can find a wide variety of diamond jewelry at affordable prices.

Shop for fashion: Israel has a growing fashion industry, and you can find a wide range of fashionable clothing, shoes, and accessories in shops and markets throughout the country. Tel Aviv is considered the fashion capital of Israel, and it's a great place to find trendy and unique fashion products.

Look for local specialties: Israel is home to a wide range of local specialties, such as olive oil, wine, Dead Sea cosmetics, and more. These products can be found in shops and markets throughout the country and are a great way to take a piece of Israel home with you.

Bargain: Bargaining is a common practice in many markets and shops in Israel. It's a great way to get a good deal on a product, but it's important to be respectful and polite when bargaining.

Be aware of the opening hours: Keep in mind that most shops and markets in Israel close early on Friday, and are closed on Saturday in observance of the Jewish Sabbath.

Tax refunds: Tourists can get a VAT (Value Added Tax) refund on purchases made in Israel by presenting their passport and the original receipt at the time of purchase. The refund can be claimed at the airport or designated refund centers before leaving the country. It's important to note that certain restrictions apply, such as a minimum purchase amount and certain exclusions, so it's best to check with the merchant or the refund center for more information.

In conclusion, Israel offers a wide range of shopping options for visitors. From traditional markets to modern malls, there is something for everyone. Some of the best shopping experiences can be found in traditional markets such as the Carmel Market in Tel Aviv, the Mahane Yehuda Market in Jerusalem, and the Shuk HaCarmel in Haifa, where you can find a variety of products such as fresh produce, spices, souvenirs, clothing, jewelry, and more. You can also find a wide range of local and handmade products and local specialties like olive oil, wine, Dead Sea cosmetics, and more. Israel is also famous for its jewelry and diamond. Shopping centers like Azrieli Center and Malha Mall in Tel Aviv and Jerusalem offer a wide range of shops, restaurants, and entertainment options, and are a great place to find international brands and products. Remember that bargaining is a common practice in many markets and shops in Israel and also be aware of the opening hours, and Tax refunds. With the right planning and preparation, you can have a great shopping experience in Israel.

Overview of the local shopping scene in Israel , including markets, boutiques, and souvenir shops

Israel offers a diverse and vibrant shopping scene, with a wide range of options for visitors to choose from. From traditional markets to modern malls, there is something for everyone.

Markets: Israel is home to many traditional markets, such as the Carmel Market in Tel Aviv, the Mahane Yehuda Market in Jerusalem, and the Shuk HaCarmel in Haifa. These markets offer a unique shopping experience, and are a great way to immerse yourself in the local culture. You can find a variety of products such as fresh produce, spices, souvenirs, clothing, jewelry, and more. Many of these markets are open-air, and offer a lively and colorful atmosphere. They are a great place to find local and handmade products, as well as a wide range of local specialties like olive oil, wine, and Dead Sea cosmetics.

Boutiques: Israel has a growing fashion industry, and you can find a wide range of fashionable clothing, shoes, and accessories in boutiques throughout the country. Tel Aviv is considered the fashion capital of

Israel, and it's a great place to find trendy and unique fashion products. There are many local and independent boutiques in Tel Aviv, which offer a wide range of products, from high-end designer wear to more affordable street-style fashion.

Souvenir shops: Israel is a popular tourist destination, and there are many souvenir shops throughout the country where you can find a wide range of products to take home as a reminder of your trip. These shops offer a wide range of products such as traditional Jewish souvenirs like the Hamsa and Star of David, Israeli flags, and postcards, as well as more unique products like olive oil, wine, Dead Sea cosmetics, and more.

Shopping centers: Israel has many modern shopping centers, such as the Azrieli Center in Tel Aviv, and the Malha Mall in Jerusalem. These centers offer a wide range of shops, restaurants, and entertainment options, and are a great place to find international brands and products. They are also a good option for those looking for a more air-conditioned and comfortable shopping experience.

Jewelry: Israel is known for its jewelry and you can find a wide range of high-quality and unique jewelry in shops and markets throughout the country. The most popular types of jewelry are the traditional Jewish jewelry, such as the Hamsa and the Star of David. Israel is also famous for its diamonds, so you can find a wide variety of diamond jewelry at affordable prices.

In conclusion, Israel offers a diverse and vibrant shopping scene, with a wide range of options for visitors to choose from. From traditional markets to modern malls, there is something for everyone. Some of the best shopping experiences can be found in traditional markets such as the Carmel Market in Tel Aviv, the Mahane Yehuda Market in Jerusalem, and the Shuk HaCarmel in Haifa. You can also find a wide range of local and handmade products and local specialties like olive oil, wine, Dead Sea cosmetics, and more. Israel is also famous for its jewelry and diamond. Shopping centers like Azrieli Center and Malha Mall in Tel Aviv and Jerusalem offer a wide range of shops, restaurants, and entertainment options, and are a great place to find international brands and products. Boutiques in Tel Aviv offer a wide range of fashionable clothing, shoes, and accessories. Souvenir shops are also available throughout the country where you can find a wide range of products to take home as a reminder of your trip. With the right planning and preparation, you can have a great shopping experience in Israel.

Chapter 10: Nightlife in Israel

Israel offers a vibrant and diverse nightlife scene, with something for everyone, from lively bars and clubs to more relaxed and intimate settings. Here is an overview of the nightlife in Israel:

Tel Aviv: Tel Aviv is known for its lively and diverse nightlife scene. The city is home to a wide range of bars, clubs, and music venues, catering to different music genres and crowds. The city's central areas like Rothschild Boulevard, Carmel Market, and Neve Tzedek are popular spots for nightlife, with many bars and clubs lining the streets. The city also has a thriving gay scene, with many gay-friendly bars and clubs.

Jerusalem: Jerusalem's nightlife scene is more relaxed and intimate compared to Tel Aviv. The city is home to a variety of bars, pubs, and clubs, with a focus on live music and cultural events. The city's Old City is a popular spot for nightlife, with many bars and clubs offering a unique and historical setting. In addition, there are many cultural events and festivals that take place throughout the year, such as the Jerusalem International Film Festival and the Jerusalem Wine Festival.

Eilat: Eilat is a popular tourist destination and is known for its lively and upbeat nightlife scene. The city is home to a variety of bars, clubs, and music venues, catering to different music genres and crowds. The city's promenade is a popular spot for nightlife, with many bars and clubs lining the streets, as well as a variety of street performances and live music.

Haifa: Haifa is a city with a more laid-back and relaxed nightlife scene, with a focus on cultural events and live music. The city is home to a variety of bars, pubs, and clubs, with many offering a unique and historical setting. The city's German Colony and

Carmel Center are popular spots for nightlife, with many bars and clubs lining the streets.

Tips for Nightlife in Israel:

·   Be aware of the dress code: Many clubs and bars in Israel have a dress code, so it's best to check before you go.

·   Be aware of the closing times: Many bars and clubs in Israel close early, usually around 2 am.

·   Be aware of the cover charge: Some bars and clubs in Israel have a cover charge, so it's best to check before you go.

- Be aware of the drinking age: The legal drinking age in Israel is 18 years old.
- Have a plan for transportation: Israel has strict drunk driving laws, and it's best to have a plan for transportation before you go out.
- Try something new: Israel offers a diverse and vibrant nightlife scene,

with something for everyone. Take the opportunity to try something new and explore different areas and venues.

In conclusion, Israel offers a vibrant and diverse nightlife scene, with something for everyone. Tel Aviv is known for its lively and diverse nightlife scene, with a focus on bars, clubs and music venues. Jerusalem's nightlife scene is more relaxed and intimate, with a focus on live music and cultural events. Eilat is known for its lively and upbeat nightlife scene, with many bars, clubs, and music venues. Haifa is a city with a more laid-back and relaxed nightlife scene, with a focus on cultural events and live music. It's important to be aware of the dress code, closing times, cover charge, and drinking age, and to have a plan for transportation. Try something new and explore different areas and venues. With the right planning and preparation, you can have a great nightlife experience in Israel.

Overview of the local nightlife scene in Israel, including bars, clubs, and live music venues

Israel offers a vibrant and diverse nightlife scene, with a wide range of options for visitors to choose from. Whether you're looking for lively bars and clubs, or more relaxed and intimate settings, there is something for everyone.

Bars: Israel is home to many bars, with a wide range of styles and crowds. Tel Aviv is known for its lively and diverse nightlife scene, with many bars, clubs and music venues. The city's central areas like Rothschild Boulevard, Carmel Market, and Neve Tzedek are popular spots for nightlife, with many bars and clubs lining the streets. Jerusalem's nightlife scene is more relaxed and intimate, with a focus on live music and cultural events. The city's Old City is a popular spot for nightlife, with many bars and clubs offering a unique and historical setting. Eilat is a popular tourist destination and is known for its lively and upbeat nightlife scene. The city's promenade is a popular spot for nightlife, with many bars and clubs lining the streets. Haifa is a city with a more laid-back and relaxed nightlife scene, with a focus on cultural events and live music. The city's German Colony and Carmel Center are popular spots for nightlife, with many bars and clubs lining the streets.

Clubs: Israel is home to many clubs, with a wide range of styles and crowds. Tel Aviv is known for its lively and diverse nightlife scene, with many clubs catering to different music genres and crowds. The city's central areas like Rothschild Boulevard, Carmel Market, and Neve Tzedek are popular spots for nightlife, with many clubs lining the streets. Jerusalem's nightlife scene is more relaxed and intimate, with a focus on live music and cultural events. The city's Old City is a popular spot for nightlife, with many clubs offering a unique and historical setting. Eilat is a popular tourist destination and is known for its lively and upbeat nightlife scene. The city's promenade is a popular spot for nightlife, with many clubs lining the streets. Haifa is a city with a more laid-back and relaxed nightlife scene, with a focus on cultural events and live music. The city's German Colony and Carmel Center are popular spots for nightlife, with many clubs lining the streets.

Live music venues: Israel is home to many live music venues, with a wide range of styles and crowds. Tel Aviv is known for its lively and diverse nightlife scene, with many live music venues catering to different music genres and crowds. The city's central areas like Rothschild Boulevard, Carmel Market, and Neve Tzedek are popular spots for nightlife, with many live music venues lining the streets. Jerusalem's nightlife scene is more relaxed and intimate, with a focus on live music and cultural events. The city's Old City is a popular spot for nightlife, with many live music venues offering a unique and historical setting. Eilat is a popular tourist destination and is known for its lively and upbeat nightlife scene. The city's promenade is a popular spot for nightlife, with many live music venues lining the streets. Haifa is a city with a more laid-back and relaxed nightlife scene, with a focus on cultural events and live music. The city's German Colony and Carmel Center are popular spots for nightlife, with many live music venues lining the streets.

In conclusion, Israel offers a vibrant and diverse nightlife scene, with a wide range of options for visitors to choose from. Whether you're looking for lively bars and clubs, or more relaxed and intimate settings, there is something for everyone. Tel Aviv is known for its lively and diverse nightlife scene, with many bars, clubs, and live music venues catering to different music genres and crowds. The city's central areas like Rothschild Boulevard, Carmel Market, and Neve Tzedek are popular spots for nightlife. Jerusalem's nightlife scene is more relaxed and intimate, with a focus on live music and cultural events. The city's Old City is a popular spot for nightlife, with many bars, clubs, and live music venues offering a unique and historical setting. Eilat is a popular tourist destination and is known for its lively and upbeat nightlife scene, with many bars, clubs, and live music venues lining the streets. Haifa is a city with a more laid-back and relaxed nightlife scene, with a focus on cultural events and live music. The city's German Colony and Carmel Center are popular spots for nightlife. It's important to research and plan ahead to make the most of your nightlife experience in Israel, and to be aware of the dress code, closing times, cover charge, and drinking age. With the right planning and preparation, you can have a great nightlife experience in Israel.

Chapter 11: Practical Information

Practical information is a crucial aspect of planning and preparing for a trip to Israel. From visa requirements to currency exchange and emergency contact information, it's important to be informed and have all necessary documents and information at hand before your trip.

Visa Requirements: Tourists visiting Israel are required to have a valid passport with at least six months remaining before expiration. Citizens of most countries, including the United States, Canada, and European Union countries, do not require a visa for stays of up to three months. However, it's always best to check with your local Israeli consulate for the most up-to-date information and visa requirements for your specific country of citizenship.

Currency: The currency used in Israel is the Israeli New Shekel (ILS or NIS). Currency exchange is available at banks, currency exchange offices, and many hotels. It's also possible to use credit cards at most places in Israel, but it's always best to have some cash on hand for smaller transactions and for places that do not accept credit cards.

Emergency contact information: It's important to have emergency contact information with you at all times during your trip to Israel. This should include the contact information for your country's embassy or consulate in Israel, as well as emergency numbers such as the police and ambulance.

Weather: Israel has a Mediterranean climate, with hot summers and mild winters. The best time to visit Israel is in the spring (April to May) or fall (September to November), when the weather is more comfortable and there are fewer tourists. It's important to bring appropriate clothing and sunscreen, as the sun can be intense, especially during the summer months.

Safety and security: Israel is generally a safe place to visit, but as with any travel destination, it's important to exercise caution and be aware of your surroundings. It's best to avoid large crowds and demonstrations and to stay informed about any potential security risks. The US Department of State and the UK Foreign and Commonwealth Office provide updated information about safety and security in Israel.

Health: Israel has high-quality healthcare and it's easy to find English-speaking doctors and hospitals. It's important to have adequate travel health insurance and to bring any necessary medication with you. It's also recommended to drink bottled water and to be cautious about eating street food.

Communication: Israel has a well-developed mobile network, and it's easy to purchase a prepaid SIM card for your phone. It's also possible to find free Wi-Fi in many places such as cafes, hotels, and public spaces.

In conclusion, practical information is a crucial aspect of planning and preparing for a trip to Israel. From visa requirements to currency exchange and emergency contact information, it's important to be informed and have all necessary documents and information at hand before your trip. It's important to check with your local Israeli consulate for the most up-to-date information and visa requirements, to have emergency contact information with you at all times, to be aware of weather and to bring appropriate clothing, to stay informed about any potential security risks and to take necessary precautions, to have adequate travel health insurance and to bring any necessary medication with you, and to be aware of the communication options available in the country. With the right planning and preparation, you can have a safe, comfortable, and enjoyable trip to Israel.

Tips on staying safe and healthy while traveling in Israel , including information on local laws and customs, medical facilities, and emergency resources

Staying safe and healthy while traveling to Israel is important for having a comfortable and enjoyable trip. It's important to be aware of local laws and customs, as well as to have information about medical facilities and emergency resources readily available.

Local laws and customs: It's important to be aware of and respect local laws and customs while in Israel. This includes being aware of and respectful of religious customs, such as dressing modestly when visiting holy sites, and avoiding public displays of affection. It's also important to be aware of and follow local laws regarding drugs, alcohol, and smoking. Breaking these laws can result in severe penalties, including imprisonment.

Medical facilities: Israel has high-quality healthcare and it's easy to find English-speaking doctors and hospitals. If you need medical attention, it's best to go to a hospital or clinic, and to have adequate travel health insurance. It's also recommended to bring any necessary medication with you and to be aware of your health and any potential risks while traveling.

Emergency resources: It's important to have emergency contact information with you at all times during your trip to Israel. This should include the contact information for your country's embassy or consulate in Israel, as well as emergency numbers such as the police, ambulance, and fire department. It's also a good idea to have a plan in place in case of an emergency and to be aware of potential risks and hazards.

Safety tips:

- Be aware of your surroundings and avoid large crowds and demonstrations
- Don't carry large amounts of cash or valuables with you
- Keep a copy of your passport and important documents in a safe place
- Avoid walking alone at night
- Be aware of the level of crime in the area where you are staying
- Be aware of local weather conditions and take necessary precautions
- Be aware of local customs and laws
- Be aware of and respect religious customs
- Be aware of and follow local laws regarding drugs, alcohol, and smoking

In conclusion, staying safe and healthy while traveling to Israel is important for having a comfortable and enjoyable trip. It's important to be aware of local laws and customs, as well as to have information about medical facilities and emergency resources readily available. Be aware of your surroundings and avoid large crowds and demonstrations, don't carry large amounts of cash or valuables with you, keep a copy of your passport and important documents in a safe place, avoid walking alone at night, be aware of the level of crime in the area where you are staying, be aware of local weather conditions and take necessary precautions, be aware of local customs and laws, be aware of and respect religious customs, and be aware of and follow local laws regarding drugs, alcohol, and smoking. With the right planning and preparation, you can have a safe and healthy trip to Israel.

Information on visas, travel insurance

Visa Requirements: Tourists visiting Israel are required to have a valid passport with at least six months remaining before expiration. Citizens of most countries, including the United States, Canada, and

European Union countries, do not require a visa for stays of up to three months. However, it's always best to check with your local Israeli consulate for the most up-to-date information and visa requirements for your specific country of citizenship. If you plan on staying longer than 3 months or plan to work or study while in Israel, you will need to apply for a visa. It's also important to have a return or onward ticket as you may be asked to present it at the border.

Travel Insurance: Travel insurance is an important aspect of planning and preparing for a trip to Israel. It's important to have adequate coverage for medical expenses, trip cancellation, and other potential travel-related risks. It's also a good idea to check if your insurance covers you for any activities you plan on doing, such as adventure sports or rental car insurance. It's also a good idea to bring a copy of your insurance policy and the contact information for the insurance company with you while traveling.

When purchasing travel insurance, it's important to read and understand the policy carefully, and to ensure that it covers all of your needs. Some things to consider when purchasing travel insurance include:

- Coverage for medical expenses and emergency medical evacuation
- Coverage for trip cancellation or interruption
- Coverage for lost or stolen luggage and personal effects
- Coverage for accidents or injuries while engaging in adventure sports
- Coverage for rental car insurance
- Coverage for travel-related risks such as terrorism or natural disasters

It's also important to inform your insurance company of your travel plans and to have the contact information for the insurance company with you while traveling. In case of an emergency, it's important to know who to contact and how to contact them.

In conclusion, obtaining a visa and getting travel insurance are important aspects of planning and preparing for a trip to Israel. It's important to check with your local Israeli consulate for the most up-to-date information and visa requirements for your specific country of citizenship, and to make sure you have adequate coverage for medical expenses, trip cancellation, and other potential travel-related risks. It's important to read and understand your insurance policy carefully and to ensure that it covers all of your needs, to inform your insurance company of your travel plans and to have the contact information for the insurance company with you while traveling. With the right planning and preparation, you can have a safe and comfortable trip to Israel.

Tips for a successful and enjoyable trip

Tips for a successful and enjoyable trip to Israel:

1. Research and plan ahead: Researching the destinations you plan on visiting and planning ahead can save you time and make your trip more enjoyable. It's important to research the best time to visit, what to pack, and what to expect. It's also a good idea to research the different regions of Israel and to plan your itinerary accordingly.

2. Learn about the culture and customs: Israel has a rich and diverse culture, and understanding the customs and traditions can make your trip more enjoyable. It's important to be respectful of religious customs, such as dressing modestly when visiting holy sites, and to be aware of and follow local laws and customs.

3. Be open to new experiences: Israel is a country with many different cultures and customs. Be open to new experiences and try new things such as trying new foods, learning about the history and culture, and immersing yourself in the local way of life.
4. Be respectful: Be respectful of the local culture and people. Showing respect for the local culture and people can go a long way in making your trip more enjoyable.
5. Learn some Hebrew: Learning some basic Hebrew can be helpful, especially when communicating with locals. Knowing a few Hebrew phrases can make it easier to navigate around the country and help you to understand the culture better.
6. Use public transportation: Israel has a well-developed public transportation system, and it's a great way to explore the country. It's also a more

budget-friendly option and a great way to meet locals.

7. Be aware of safety: Israel is a generally safe place to visit, but as with any travel destination, it's important to exercise caution and be aware of your surroundings. Be aware of potential risks and hazards and always have emergency contact information with you.

8. Stay connected: Stay connected with friends and family back home, and share your experiences with them. Use social media, or other communication tools to keep in touch, it's also a great way to document your trip.

9. Be flexible: Traveling can sometimes require a more flexible approach. Be prepared for unexpected changes in plans, and have backup options in case things don't go as planned. Remember to take time to relax and enjoy the journey, and don't put too much pressure on yourself.

10. Have fun: Remember to have fun and enjoy your trip! Israel has a lot to offer, from its rich history and culture to its beautiful landscapes, so take the time to relax and enjoy the journey.

In conclusion, Israel is a country with a rich and diverse culture, history and landscapes, and a successful and enjoyable trip requires research, planning, and an open mind. It's important to be respectful of the local culture and people, to learn some Hebrew, to use public transportation, to be aware of safety and to have emergency contact information with you. Be open to new experiences and try new things, be flexible, stay connected with friends and family, and most importantly, have fun. With the right planning and preparation, you can have a successful and enjoyable trip to Israel. Remember to take the time to relax, explore and immerse yourself in the local culture, and make unforgettable memories.

Dealing with unexpected situations

Dealing with unexpected situations while traveling to Israel can be challenging, but with the right mindset and preparation, it's possible to navigate through them and make the most of your trip.

1. Be prepared: Before you travel, it's important to be prepared for unexpected situations. This includes researching the destinations you plan on visiting, understanding the local culture and customs, and having emergency contact information with you. Having a basic understanding of Hebrew and the local currency can also be helpful.

2. Have a plan: Having a plan in place for dealing with unexpected situations can make it easier to navigate through them. This includes knowing the location of the nearest embassy or consulate, having emergency contact information with you, and having a

plan for how to communicate with loved ones in case of an emergency.

3. Stay calm: In the event of an unexpected situation, it's important to stay calm and think clearly. Panicking will only make the situation worse and make it harder to think clearly and make decisions.

4. Seek help: If you need help, don't hesitate to ask for it. Whether it's from local authorities, embassy staff, or other travelers, it's important to seek help if you need it.

5. Be flexible: Unexpected situations can disrupt your travel plans and it's important to be flexible. Be prepared to change your plans and have backup options in case things don't go as planned.

6. Keep a positive attitude: Maintaining a positive attitude can make a big difference when dealing with unexpected situations. Instead of focusing on the negatives, try to find

the silver lining in the situation and make the most of it.

7. Learn from the experience: Unexpected situations can be frustrating and stressful, but they can also be an opportunity to learn and grow. Take the time to reflect on the experience and learn from it.

8. Have travel insurance: Having travel insurance can provide peace of mind and financial protection in case of unexpected situations such as medical emergencies, trip cancellations, and lost or stolen luggage.

In conclusion, dealing with unexpected situations while traveling to Israel can be challenging, but with the right mindset and preparation, it's possible to navigate through them and make the most of your trip. It's important to be prepared, have a plan, stay calm, seek help, be flexible, keep a positive attitude, learn from the experience and have travel insurance. Remember, unexpected situations are a part of travel, and with the right approach, you can turn them into positive experiences.

Chapter 12: Christian Pilgrimage in Israel

Christian pilgrimage in Israel is a journey of faith and spiritual significance, where visitors can walk in the footsteps of Jesus and experience the holy sites where many of the events of the Bible took place. The Holy Land has been a destination for Christian pilgrims for centuries, and continues to be an important pilgrimage site for Christians of all denominations today.

The most popular Christian pilgrimage sites in Israel include:

1. The Church of the Holy Sepulchre in Jerusalem: This is one of the most important Christian pilgrimage sites in the world, believed to be the site of Jesus' crucifixion, burial, and resurrection. The church is shared by several Christian denominations, including the Greek Orthodox, Roman

Catholic, and Armenian Apostolic churches.

2. The Sea of Galilee: This is the place where Jesus spent much of his ministry and performed many of his miracles, including the feeding of the 5,000 and the calming of the storm. Visitors can take a boat ride on the sea, and visit the Church of the Multiplication of Loaves and Fishes and the Church of the Beatitudes.

3. The Mount of Beatitudes: Located on the northwest shore of the Sea of Galilee, this is the traditional site of the Sermon on the Mount, where Jesus delivered the Beatitudes.

4. The Church of the Annunciation in Nazareth: This is the site where the angel Gabriel is believed to have appeared to Mary and announced that she would give birth to Jesus.

5. The Jordan River: This is the site where Jesus was baptized by John the

Baptist, and is considered a place of spiritual renewal and purification.

6. The Church of All Nations in the Garden of Gethsemane: This is the site where Jesus is believed to have prayed before his arrest and crucifixion. The church is also known as the Church of the Agony and is located at the foot of the Mount of Olives.

7. The Basilica of the Agony in Ein Karem: This is the site of the first miracle of Jesus, when he turned water into wine at the wedding in Cana.

8. The Church of St. Peter in Gallicantu: This is the site where Jesus was held prisoner before his trial and crucifixion. It is also believed to be the site of the high priest Caiaphas' house.

9. The Church of St. Anne in Jerusalem: This is the site where Anne, the mother of Mary, was born and raised.

10.   The Church of St. John the Baptist in Ein Kerem: This is the site where John the Baptist was born and raised.

In addition to visiting these pilgrimage sites, many Christian tour groups also include visits to other important historical and cultural sites in Israel such as Masada, Caesarea and the City of David.

When planning a Christian pilgrimage to Israel, it's important to research the different tour options and to choose one that best meets your spiritual and travel needs. Some tour groups offer a more traditional pilgrimage experience, with a focus on prayer and reflection, while others offer a more historical and cultural experience, with a focus on learning about the history and culture of the region.

It's also important to consider the time of year when planning your pilgrimage. The best time to visit Israel is during the spring and fall, when the weather is mild and comfortable. During the summer months, temperatures can be extremely hot, making it difficult to visit some of the outdoor sites.

When visiting the pilgrimage sites, it's important to be respectful of the local culture and customs, and to dress modestly. Many of the holy sites have specific dress codes and it's important to follow them to show respect to the other visitors and those who use these places of worship.

Another important aspect of Christian pilgrimage in Israel is the opportunity to deepen one's spiritual journey through prayer, reflection, and meditation. Many tour groups offer opportunities for mass and other religious services at the pilgrimage sites, and many also include time for personal reflection and meditation.

For those who are interested in a more in-depth spiritual experience, there are also retreat centers and monasteries located throughout Israel that offer spiritual retreats and programs. These can include guided meditations, spiritual teachings, and opportunities for personal reflection and growth.

Finally, it's important to note that Israel is a relatively safe destination for travelers, but like any place, it's important to be aware of your surroundings and to take precautions for your personal safety. This includes staying in well-lit and populated areas, being aware of your belongings, and avoiding large crowds or demonstrations.

In conclusion, a Christian pilgrimage to Israel is an incredibly powerful and meaningful experience, a journey of faith and spiritual significance where visitors can walk in the footsteps of Jesus and experience the holy sites where many of the events of the Bible took place. It's important to research and plan ahead, to be respectful of the local culture and customs, and to be prepared for unexpected situations. With the right preparation and mindset, a

Christian pilgrimage to Israel can be a life-changing and unforgettable experience.

Chapter 13: Itineraries

When planning a Christian pilgrimage to Israel, it's important to consider the different itineraries available and to choose one that best meets your spiritual and travel needs. Here are a few sample itineraries to consider:

Classic Christian Pilgrimage: This itinerary includes visits to the most important Christian pilgrimage sites in Israel, such as the Church of the Holy Sepulchre in Jerusalem, the Sea of Galilee, the Mount of Beatitudes, the Church of the Annunciation in Nazareth, and the Jordan River. It also includes visits to other historical and cultural sites such as Masada, Caesarea, and the City of David. This itinerary is ideal for those who are looking for a traditional pilgrimage experience, with a focus on prayer and reflection.

Historical and Cultural Pilgrimage: This itinerary includes visits to the same

Christian pilgrimage sites as the classic itinerary, but with a focus on learning about the history and culture of the region. This itinerary also includes visits to museums, archaeological sites, and other historical landmarks. This itinerary is ideal for those who are interested in learning more about the history and culture of Israel and the Middle East.

Spiritual Retreat: This itinerary includes visits to the same Christian pilgrimage sites as the classic itinerary, but also includes time for personal reflection, meditation, and spiritual growth. This itinerary includes stays at retreat centers and monasteries, and includes guided meditations, spiritual teachings, and opportunities for personal reflection and growth. This itinerary is ideal for those who are looking for a more in-depth spiritual experience.

Custom Itinerary: For those who have specific interests or needs, it's also possible to create a custom itinerary. This can include visits to specific pilgrimage sites, activities or experiences that align with personal interests and preferences, and can be tailored to the time and budget available.

When planning your itinerary, it's important to consider the time of year you plan to visit Israel, as the weather and crowds can vary significantly depending on the season. The best time to visit Israel is during the spring and fall, when the weather is mild and comfortable. During the summer months, temperatures can be extremely hot, making it difficult to visit some of the outdoor sites.

It's also important to note that while these itineraries provide a general idea of what to expect, they are not set in stone. Many tour groups and pilgrimage organizers are open to making adjustments and accommodations to suit the needs of their clients. Therefore, it's important to communicate your preferences and needs to your tour organizer or guide, and to be open to making adjustments as necessary.

In conclusion, there are many different itineraries available for Christian pilgrimage in Israel, each offering a unique experience. It's important to consider your spiritual and travel needs and preferences, and to choose an itinerary that will provide the most meaningful and enjoyable experience for you. With the right itinerary and the right mindset, a Christian pilgrimage to Israel can be a life-changing and unforgettable experience.

- Suggested itineraries for different lengths of stay and interests, including options for solo travelers, families, and couples.
1. A 3-day itinerary for solo travelers:
- Day 1: Visit the Church of the Holy Sepulchre in Jerusalem, the Western Wall, and the Dome of the Rock.
- Day 2: Take a day trip to the Sea of Galilee and visit the Church of the Multiplication of Loaves and Fishes, the Church of the Beatitudes, and the Mount of Beatitudes.

- Day 3: Visit the Church of the Annunciation in Nazareth, the Jordan River, and the Basilica of the Agony in Ein Karem.
2. A 5-day itinerary for families:
- Day 1: Visit the Church of the Holy Sepulchre in Jerusalem, the Western Wall, and the Dome of the Rock.
- Day 2: Take a day trip to the Sea of Galilee and visit the Church of the Multiplication of Loaves and Fishes, the Church of the Beatitudes, and the Mount of Beatitudes.
- Day 3: Visit the Church of the Annunciation in Nazareth, the Jordan River, and the Basilica of the Agony in Ein Karem.
- Day 4: Take a day trip to Masada and the Dead Sea, and visit the Ein Gedi National Park.
- Day 5: Visit the City of David, the Western Wall Tunnels, and the Jerusalem Archaeological Park.
3. A 7-day itinerary for couples:

- Day 1: Visit the Church of the Holy Sepulchre in Jerusalem, the Western Wall, and the Dome of the Rock.
- Day 2: Take a day trip to the Sea of Galilee and visit the Church of the Multiplication of Loaves and Fishes, the Church of the Beatitudes, and the Mount of Beatitudes.
- Day 3: Visit the Church of the Annunciation in Nazareth, the Jordan River, and the Basilica of the Agony in Ein Karem.
- Day 4: Take a day trip to Masada and the Dead Sea, and visit the Ein Gedi National Park.
- Day 5: Visit the City of David, the Western Wall Tunnels, and the Jerusalem Archaeological Park.
- Day 6: Take a day trip to Jaffa, Acre and Caesarea.
- Day 7: Visit the Israel Museum, the Holocaust Museum, and the market in the old city of Jerusalem.

4. A 10-day itinerary for spiritual travelers:
- Day 1: Visit the Church of the Holy Sepulchre in Jerusalem, the Western Wall, and the Dome of the Rock.
- Day 2: Take a day trip to the Sea of Galilee and visit the Church of the Multiplication of Loaves and Fishes, the Church of the Beatitudes, and the Mount of Beatitudes.
- Day 3: Visit the Church of the Annunciation in Nazareth, the Jordan River, and the Basilica of the Agony in Ein Karem.
- Day 4: Take a day trip to Masada and the Dead Sea , and visit the Ein Gedi National Park.
- Day 5: Visit the City of David, the Western Wall Tunnels, and the Jerusalem Archaeological Park.
- Day 6: Spend the day at a spiritual retreat center in Jerusalem, participating in guided meditations and spiritual teachings.

- Day 7: Visit the Church of All Nations and the Garden of Gethsemane.
- Day 8: Take a day trip to the Monastery of the Temptation in Jericho and the Monastery of St. George in Wadi Qelt.
- Day 9: Visit the Church of the Nativity in Bethlehem and the Grotto of the Nativity.
- Day 10: Spend the last day in Jerusalem, visiting the Church of the Pater Noster and the Church of the Dominus Flevit.
- Please note that this is a sample itinerary and that depending on the time of the year, the opening hours and availability of the sites may change. Therefore, it is important to check the schedule of the sites before planning your trip and make adjustments accordingly. Also, these itineraries are just suggestions and can be adjusted to suit the different needs and interests of the travelers.

Additionally, it's important to consider the physical capabilities and mobility of the travelers when planning the itinerary, and to make adjustments as necessary. For example, for those with limited mobility, it may be best to focus on visiting the pilgrimage sites in Jerusalem and Nazareth, and to avoid sites that involve a lot of walking or climbing.

It's also important to consider the budget when planning the itinerary, as some activities and accommodations may be more expensive than others. For those on a tight budget, it may be best to focus on free activities and to look for budget-friendly accommodation options.

Finally, it's important to keep in mind that while the pilgrimage sites are the main focus of the trip, it's also important to take time to experience the local culture and way of life. This can include visiting local markets, trying local foods, and interacting with the local people.

This will help to create a more well-rounded and meaningful experience for the travelers.

In conclusion, planning a Christian pilgrimage to Israel requires careful consideration of the different itineraries available, the physical capabilities and mobility of the travelers, the budget, and the interests and needs of the travelers. By keeping these factors in mind and being open to making adjustments as necessary, it is possible to create a personalized and meaningful itinerary that will make for a truly unforgettable experience.

Final thoughts and next steps

A Christian pilgrimage to Israel is a unique and meaningful experience that offers an opportunity to deepen one's faith and connect with the land where Jesus lived, walked and preached. It's a journey that can be both challenging and rewarding, and requires careful planning and preparation.

When planning a pilgrimage, it's important to consider the different itineraries available, and to choose one that best meets your spiritual and travel needs. It's also important to consider the time of year, budget, and the physical capabilities and mobility of the travelers.

It's also important to keep in mind that while the pilgrimage sites are the main focus of the trip, it's also important to take time to experience the local culture and way of life. This can include visiting local markets, trying local foods, and interacting with the local people.

When it comes to practical matters, it's important to research and plan for the necessary travel documents, such as visas and travel insurance. It's also important to be aware of the local laws and customs, and to be respectful of the local culture and customs.

Finally, it's important to stay safe and healthy while traveling. This includes being aware of local emergency resources and medical facilities, and taking necessary precautions to ensure the safety and well-being of the travelers.

In conclusion, a Christian pilgrimage to Israel is a unique and meaningful experience that offers an opportunity to deepen one's faith and connect with the land where Jesus lived, walked and preached. With careful planning and preparation, it is possible to create a personalized and meaningful itinerary that will make for a truly unforgettable experience.

The next step is to research and choose a reputable tour operator or pilgrimage organizer that can help you plan and organize your trip. They can assist you with all the practical matters and can also provide you with a knowledgeable guide who can help you navigate the different pilgrimage sites and help you gain a deeper understanding of the historical, cultural, and spiritual significance of the places you will be visiting.

Another important step is to start reading and learning about the places you will be visiting, the history, and culture, it will help you to understand the context and background of what you'll be experiencing.

Finally, be open to new experiences, be flexible, and have an open mind. Remember, a Christian pilgrimage is not just about visiting the sites, but it's also about the journey and the spiritual growth that comes with it.

THE END

Made in the USA
Las Vegas, NV
01 April 2023

70007070R00095